study guide WITH PROGRAMED UNITS

TO ACCOMPANY KAGAN AND HAVEMANN'S

psychology: an introduction

SECOND EDITION

ROBERT B. McCALL

The Fels Research Institute and Antioch College

ERNEST HAVEMANN

 HARCOURT BRACE JOVANOVICH, INC.

New York   Chicago   San Francisco   Atlanta

Cover design by Corita Kent.

TO THE INSTRUCTOR

This *Study Guide* has been prepared as an aid for the student; it is designed to assist him in mastering the introductory course material in three ways. First, the *Guide* presents a summary of the basic concepts of the text chapters, thus ensuring that the student does not slight an important topic. This summary, however, is not exhaustive; the student must study the text for the details and context of these concepts. Second, the *Guide* provides the student with feedback on his acquisition and retention of the material. Third, the *Guide* allows the student to utilize the research methods of psychology in practical applications of the principles he has studied.

Each chapter of the *Guide* has three sections. The first section consists of a programed unit that introduces the basic vocabulary and essential ideas of the subject matter. It also provides a framework for these ideas into which the student can fit the details, examples, and context that the text offers. The programed unit can be worked before or after the chapter is read, or the student may wish to work it twice. At a later time the programed unit can be used to review for examinations.

The second section of each chapter is a self-test of twenty multiple-choice items. Since these items cover some material not touched upon in the pro-
gramed unit, the student should take the self-test after studying the text chapter and not after having finished only the programed unit (although a review of that unit before taking the test would be helpful).

The final section of each chapter contains exercises that allow the student to advance beyond mere memorization of material and to deal actively with some of the fundamental principles. In accordance with this goal, several of the questions in the exercises cannot be answered objectively and require the student to justify his response. Some items ask the student to apply what he knows to new situations that are not represented in the text. Finally, a few items request the student to collect informal data on a given concept and to interpret the results in terms of the material in the text. These exercises may form the basis of a discussion-laboratory session, or the student may carry out the experiments on his own.

A debt of gratitude is owed to Jayne Hamilton, Joanne Peterson, and Jack Vincent for their help in typing and proofreading the manuscript and to The Fels Research Institute and The Fels Fund of Philadelphia for their support.

Robert B. McCall   Ernest Havemann

TO THE STUDENT

This *Guide* has been prepared to supplement — though not replace — your textbook. Each of the *Guide* chapters, which correspond to the textbook chapters, contains three sections: a programed unit, a self-test, and exercises. These sections provide assistance in particular ways. First, the programed unit presents the basic vocabulary and
fundamental concepts that you will encounter in the text. It also provides a summary of the material in the text chapter and reflects the organization of the chapter. Second, the self-tests measure your mastery of the material presented in this *Guide* as well as the material presented in your text. Third, the exercises offer you an opportunity

to apply the methods and principles of psychology in your own experiments and problem solving situations.

The programed unit may be used either as a preview or as a review of the chapter in your text — or as both. It cannot be used as a substitute for the text chapter, since not all of the concepts presented in your text are found in the *Guide*. The programed unit is composed of a series of short steps called "frames," each of which generally introduces a concept and requires you to make a response in the form of a fill-in-the-blank statement about the concept. Scattered throughout the unit are review frames that test your retention of concepts already presented.

To the right of each blank in the frames you will find the correct answer printed in the margin. As you work the unit keep the answers covered with a sheet of paper until each blank in a frame has been filled in. Then pull the paper far enough down to uncover the correct answer (or answers). Since learning is reinforced by having to recall and write down a term or concept, you are encouraged to take the time to respond in actual writing rather than by only mentally responding and looking across to the printed answer. There are some frames in which you are asked to label parts of a diagram that has been presented with labels on a preceding page. Of course, this task will be of greatest benefit to you if you avoid looking back at the answers until you have completed the labeling. The same advice applies to the review frames — try not to look back over the preceding material to obtain the answers.

As you work through the programed units you will find that they possess certain characteristics:

1. The concepts are presented in a series of *small steps* that follow a systematic *sequential organization.*

2. There is some *repetition* of concepts to give you more than one trial in learning an item and to give you practice in recalling it.

3. You gain immediate *feedback* on the progress of your learning, because the answers are readily available and the frequent review items check your retention.

4. You are required to *respond actively* to each item rather than just experience it passively. This tends to keep your attention fixed on the material.

After you have completed the programed unit and a thorough study of the corresponding chapter in the text, you are ready to take the self-test. The self-test should *not* be taken after studying only the programed unit, because the questions in the test are taken directly from the textbook and include some material not found in the more concise programed units.

The self-test consists of twenty multiple-choice questions that sample the concepts in the chapter. Although the questions cannot provide a complete check on your mastery of the material, they do represent a fair selection of the basic concepts. Answers to the questions may be found in a key following each self-test. Use your score on the self-tests to determine what concepts require further study. Review of the self-tests and programed units can be excellent preparation for examinations.

The last section of each chapter in the *Guide* is composed of exercises, which enable you to apply the concepts you have studied to new situations and to make creative use of what you have learned. Once again, these exercises will be of greatest benefit to you if you do not return to the text to recall material (except when you are directed to do so). Sometimes the answers to the questions accompanying the exercises will not be obvious. In that event, answer as best you can but be sure to explain or justify your response. The exercises requiring a small experimental observation will give you an opportunity to acquire a sense of the scientific basis of psychology. Of course, actual psychological experimentation is performed on a much wider and more intricate scale, but these items will be sufficient to convey the general procedure.

To summarize, there are three sections to each chapter in the *Guide*: a programed unit, a self-test, and one or more exercises. The programed unit may be worked before or after studying the text chapter or both before *and* after. When you feel you are prepared after studying the text to take a test on the material, proceed with the self-test. After checking your errors and restudying points that you missed, go on to the exercises. If used properly, the *Guide* will facilitate and enrich your comprehension of the contents of the textbook.

CONTENTS

CHAPTER 1

THE scope and goals of psychology

programed unit

1. *Psychology* is the science that systematically studies and attempts to explain observable behavior and its relationship to the unseen mental processes that go on inside the organism and to external events in the environment. Notice that an incredibly wide range of behavior and mental activity is studied by the science of _____.

    psychology

2. This definition indicates that psychology studies the behavior of *organisms*. That is, it includes within its scope the behavior of all animal species, not only human beings. As its name implies, the special field of comparative psychology studies the relationship between the behavior of different _____.

    organisms

3. The object of psychological study is *behavior*. Your nervousness before an examination, the actions of children at play, and the thinking processes involved in solving a mathematical problem are all examples of _____.

    behavior

4. Behavior may be actions that can be easily observed. Such behavior is termed *overt*. Speaking and performing a piano concerto both constitute _____ behavior.

    overt

5. But psychologists also study unobservable mental processes, which are called *covert* behavior. The thinking that guides our speech and the motives that lead us to play the concerto in front of a large audience are types of _____ behavior.

    covert

6. Psychology studies and attempts to explain the relationship between observable actions and unseen mental processes, or between _____

    overt

    and _____ behavior.

    covert

7. In addition, psychologists are frequently concerned with the relationship between behavior and *external events* in the environment. The science of psychology studies the relationship between observable, or _____,   overt

   and unobservable, or _____, behavior and between be-   covert

   havior and _____ _____.   external events

8. One of the goals of psychology is to *understand* behavior. When psychologists can satisfactorily explain how and under what conditions

   a behavior occurs, it can be said that they _____   understand
   that behavior.

9. Another goal of psychology is to *predict* behavior. Given certain conditions, psychologists want to be able to state precisely what behavior

   will occur. That is, they want to be able to _____   predict
   behavioral events.

10. The two goals are closely related. If one thoroughly understands a

    particular behavior, then one should be able to _____ it.   predict

11. However, if a psychologist is able to predict a behavior, it is not necessarily true that he understands it. For instance, some people have nervous twitches that occur regularly every few seconds. Psychologists

    can _____ their occurrence, but they may not be able to   predict

    explain them sufficiently to say that they _____   understand
    why the twitches occur.

12. The science of psychology is *empirical*. This means that it is based on controlled experiments and on observations made with the greatest possible precision and objectivity. The quality that distinguishes psychology from nonscientific attempts to understand and predict behavior

    is that it is _____.   empirical

13. Psychology is a scientific discipline because it employs the same method as the natural sciences in the pursuit of its goals. Controlled experiments and precise and objective observations classify psychology as an

    _____ science.   empirical

14. *Review*
    a. Psychologists study the _____ of man and other   behavior

       _____.   organisms
    b. Psychologists are concerned with the relationship between observa-

       ble, or _____, behavior and the unseen mental processes   overt

       that go on inside the organism, known as _____ behavior.   covert
    c. An additional task for psychology is the study of the relationship

between behavior and _____ _____ in the environment.   external events

d. The goals of psychology are to _____ and _____ behavior.   understand
predict

e. The methods of psychology classify it as an _____ science.   empirical

15. One of the earliest modern psychologists was *Wilhelm Wundt,* who founded the first experimental psychology laboratory in Leipzig, Germany, in 1879. Because of this contribution, the "father of experimental psychology" is _____ _____.   Wilhelm Wundt

16. In his laboratory, Wundt studied the structure or contents of conscious experience. He and his followers started the *structural* school of psychology. The sensations, images, and feelings of conscious experience were the topics of study for the _____ school of psychology.   structural

17. Wundt's method was *introspection.* A trained subject was presented with certain simple stimuli and asked to report his sensations, images, and feelings. This looking inward at one's conscious experiences is known as _____.   introspection

18. By today's standards Wundt's procedures were crude, but he did attempt to study behavior in a *systematic* fashion. That is, Wundt presented stimuli in an orderly manner and observed the subject's report of what he experienced. Thus, in addition to establishing the first experimental laboratory, Wundt's major contribution to psychology was his _____ study of behavior.   systematic

19. The first experimental psychologist, _____, began the _____ school of psychology, which in a _____ fashion studied the contents of consciousness by the method of _____.   Wundt
structural, systematic
introspection

20. Another early psychologist was *Francis Galton.* Galton was interested in various physical and mental abilities. He wanted to determine the precise role of heredity (as opposed to environment) in producing human abilities. An early student of heredity and human abilities was _____ _____.   Francis Galton

21. Galton was primarily interested in *individual differences,* the ways in which people differ from one another. Galton believed that heredity was mainly responsible for these _____ _____.   individual differences

22. Thus, while we remember Wundt for his laboratory and his systematic method of study, we remember Galton for his emphasis on _____ _____.

individual

differences

23. *William James,* the most prominent of the early American psychologists, believed psychology should be defined as the "science of mental life." He was interested in human goals, habits, religious feelings, emotions, and mental disturbances. The functions and dynamics of the thinking mind were of primary importance to _____ _____.

William James

24. The object of study for James was *mental life.* He thought that among the most important human characteristics were the attempt to attain various goals in life and the mental activity that accompanied this pursuit. In short, James was interested in _____ _____.

mental life

25. James established the *functional* school of psychology. This school emphasized the functions of mental life, such as seeking goals, adjusting to new environments, choosing between alternatives, and so on. In contrast to Wundt's _____ school, James initiated the _____ school of psychology.

structural

functional

26. The first prominent American psychologist, _____, studied the_____aspects of _____ _____.

James

functional, mental life

27. A more recent American psychologist was *John Watson.* Watson rebelled against the study of such covert processes as consciousness; indeed he believed that psychologists should instead examine only overt behavior. The only scientific subject matter of psychology was observable behavior as far as _____ _____ was concerned.

John Watson

28. Watson's emphasis on observable acts became known as *behaviorism.* The overriding concern with overt as opposed to covert behavior in psychology is called _____.

behaviorism

29. Watson believed that everything we do is predetermined by our past experiences; to him all human behavior was a series of events in which a *stimulus,* some event in the environment, produces a *response,* an observable muscular movement or physiological reaction. According to behaviorism, the smooth stream of human behavior is nothing more than a series of _____ and _____ pairs.

stimulus, response

30. Watson believed that through *conditioning,* a type of learning, almost any stimulus could be made to produce almost any kind of response. In fact, Watson boasted that he could take any dozen babies at birth

and turn them into anything he wished—doctor, lawyer, beggar, or thief—by the process of _____ alone.

conditioning

31. A contemporary psychologist who has continued and expanded the principles of behaviorism is *B. F. Skinner*. The emphasis on the association of stimuli with overt responses through conditioning began with Watson and has been continued by ____ ____ _____.

B. F. Skinner

32. *Review*

   a. The first experimental psychology laboratory was established by _____. He studied the structure or contents of consciousness by the method of _____ and began the _____ school of psychology. Although Wundt did not discover any profound laws of behavior, we will remember him for his disciplined and _____ methods of investigation.

Wundt

introspection

structural

systematic

   b. Another early psychologist, _____, was interested in human abilities and in measuring _____ _____.

Galton

individual
   differences

   c. The first prominent American psychologist, _____, studied the functions of human _____ _____. He established the _____ school of psychology.

James

mental life

functional

   d. More recently, _____ argued that psychological study should be restricted to observable behavior. This school of thought, known as _____, suggests that most of man's behavior is based on the associations between a _____ and a _____ that are built up by the learning process of _____.

Watson

behaviorism

stimulus

response

conditioning

   e. A modern proponent of behaviorism is _____.

Skinner

   f. Historically, the role of heredity in behavior was promoted by _____, while the importance of learning was the hallmark of _____ and Skinner.

Galton

Watson

   g. Both Wundt and James studied consciousness, but Wundt was concerned with the _____ aspects, while James focused on the _____ aspects of conscious experience.

structural

functional

   h. Both Wundt and James relied on the method of _____ whereas this approach was rejected by _____, who restricted psychological study to observable events.

introspection

Watson

33. The behaviorists have done much to make psychology an objective study of behavior. But more recently much of what the behaviorists ruled out of psychology is again being studied. For example, one new school of thought is *cognitive psychology*. Its followers maintain that human behavior cannot be explained in full by simple stimulus-response connections. Instead they emphasize cognition, or the importance of the mind in directing behavior. The proposition that the mind actively processes the information it receives, makes comparisons and decisions, and directs responses is the basic tenet of _____   cognitive

_____.   psychology

34. A second new school is *humanistic psychology*. As its name suggests, discerning the qualities that distinguish human beings from other animals is the main concern of _____ _____.   humanistic psychology

35. The school of *psychoanalysis,* founded by Sigmund Freud, is another movement that has had a profound influence on psychological thinking. Around the turn of the century, Freud founded the school of

_____.   psychoanalysis

36. One of Freud's great insights into human personality was the discovery of how it is influenced by *unconscious processes,* especially motives of which we are unaware. Hidden sexual motives are examples of

_____ _____.   unconscious processes

37. *Review*
   a. Three contemporary schools of thought can be discerned in psychology in addition to behaviorism. Emphasis on the importance of the mind as an executive in governing behavior characterizes the

   position of _____ _____.   cognitive psychology
   b. The factors that distinguish man from other animals are the focus

   of _____ _____.   humanistic psychology

   c. Freud's school of _____ contributed   psychoanalysis

   the concept of motives of which we are unaware, or _____   unconscious

   _____.   processes

38. The most powerful of the empirical methods of contemporary psychology is the scientific *experiment,* a careful and rigidly controlled examination of cause and effect. The psychologist can often determine that certain conditions will result in specific measurable changes in the

behavior of his subjects by conducting an _____.   experiment

39. Every experiment is an attempt to discover relationships among certain conditions or events that can be changed or that result from such

changes. These conditions, events, and resulting behavioral changes are called *variables*. If a psychologist wants to know the influence of food deprivation on the number of correct responses an animal makes to obtain food, food deprivation and the number of correct responses are the _____.

    variables

40. Any condition controlled by the experimenter, because it is set up independently of anything the subject does or does not do, is called an *independent variable*. If the experimenter deprives some animals of food for twelve hours and others for twenty-four hours, the amount of food deprivation is said to be the _____ _____.

    independent

    variable

41. The change in the subject's behavior that results from a change in an independent variable is called the *dependent variable*. In the example discussed above, the number of correct responses that the animals make as a result of different amounts of food deprivation is the _____ _____.

    dependent

    variable

42. Suppose a psychologist designs the following experiment: One man is angered by and assaults another (both are confederates of the experimenter) in the presence of others, and the observers are asked either three or twelve months later to describe the event, as a witness would do in a court hearing. The number of correct recollections of the event would be the _____ _____, while the length of time before the "trial" (three or twelve months) is the condition controlled by the experimenter, or the _____ _____.

    dependent variable

    independent

    variable

43. Often a psychologist attempts to determine whether the presence of a certain condition influences some behavior. For example, the experimenter might want to know whether a specific drug has any effect on learning. Suppose that twenty college men receive the drug and are then given a learning task. This group is called the *experimental group*. The group that receives the experimental manipulation, in this case the drug, is the _____ _____.

    experimental group

44. However, to evaluate the effects of the drug there must be a *control group*, which is similar in every way to the experimental group except that it does not receive the drug. Thus twenty additional college men—similar to the experimental group in age, grades in school, and learning ability—would be given an injection of a neutral substance, not the drug, and then given the same learning task. They would constitute the _____ _____.

    control group

45. Notice that the men in the control group were also given an injection, but of a neutral substance. If this was not done, any difference between the groups' performance on the learning task might be associated with the men's knowledge that they were drugged or not drugged and not a result of the drug itself. When subjects are prevented from knowing whether they belong to the experimental or control group, the experimenter is said to use the *single blind* technique. If some college students are given marijuana and others a special "neutral" cigarette that looks and tastes like marijuana, and then members of both groups are asked to perform on a test that measures driving skill,

the experimental method used is the _____ _____   single blind
technique.

46. However, if the experimenter knew which subjects were given marijuana and which were not, his judgment of their driving performance might be affected by this knowledge. A method that overcomes this difficulty is to have a third individual administer the marijuana and the experimenter evaluate the driving performance of all subjects without knowing whether they belong to the experimental or control group. This experimental method is the *double blind technique*. In the drug experiment described above, if the individual who administered the drug and the neutral substance and the experimenter who scored the groups' learning performance were different people who did not communicate,

the experiment would involve the _____ _____   double blind
technique.

47. When the subjects do not know which group they belong to, experimental or control, the experimental method used is the _____   single

_____ technique. When neither the subjects nor the experimenter observing the dependent variable know which group the subjects belong to, the method is the _____ _____   double blind
technique.

48. *Review*
   a. The most powerful empirical method of psychology is the scientific

   _____.   experiment
   b. An experiment is a rigidly controlled procedure to determine the

   cause and effect relationships between two or more _____.   variables
   c. Usually the experimenter deliberately manipulates and controls

   a condition or event, called the _____   independent

   _____, and then observes the effects of the ex-   variable
   perimental condition on some aspect of behavior, known as the

   _____ _____.   dependent variable
   d. Often an experiment must compare the behavior of one group that is

subject to the experimental condition, the _____ | experimental

_____, with the behavior of a similar group that is not sub- | group

ject to the condition, the _____ _____. | control group

e. If the subjects do not know which group they belong to, the experi-

mental method used is the _____ _____ technique. | single blind

f. If neither the subjects nor the experimenter observing the dependent variable knows which group the subjects belong to, the method is

the _____ _____ technique. | double blind

49. But the experiment is not the only way for an empirical science to observe behavior. *Naturalistic observation* is a method in which careful records of behavior are made in a natural setting. Going to a nursery school and systematically recording the type and frequency of the

spontaneous play behavior of children would constitute _____ | naturalistic

_____. | observation

50. The major difference between the two methods is that certain conditions are manipulated and controlled by the scientist in one but not in the other. When the researcher systematically controls and manipulates the conditions under which the observations take place, he

performs an _____. In contrast, if the researcher | experiment
makes his observations without manipulating conditions, this is called

_____ _____. | naturalistic observation

51. Another method of psychology is the use of *tests*, which measure a certain type of behavior. The College Boards and the final exam in

this course are both _____. | tests

52. The *interview* is a structured conversation, sometimes used by psychologists to gather data. Kinsey's well-known reports on human sexual

behavior were the result of personal _____ with | interviews
many people.

53. A *questionnaire* is a series of written questions to which people are asked to respond. The questionnaire is especially useful in gathering information quickly from large numbers of people. Political pollsters

frequently survey opinions with the _____ | questionnaire
technique.

54. *Review*
Psychological research uses several methods of making objective and precise observations. These methods include 1) the control and manipu-

lation of research conditions in the _____; 2) the | experiment observation of behavior in an unaltered setting called _____   naturalistic

_____; 3) the administration of psychological   observation

_____, such as the College Boards; 4) the giving of a personal   tests

_____; and 5) the gathering of information with a   interview

written _____.   questionnaire

55. Psychologists who are solely interested in increasing our scientific knowledge of behavior approach psychology as a *pure science.* Since these people are not primarily concerned with the possible applications of this knowledge but mainly in gathering scientific information, they

study psychology as a _____ _____.   pure science

56. Other psychologists prefer to make practical applications of the empirical facts obtained by pure scientists. They approach psychology as an *applied science.* Psychologists who work in schools, give vocational guidance, design machinery for efficient human operation, survey public opinion, and diagnose and treat behavior problems (clinical psychologists) practice psychology as an _____ _____.   applied science

57. Psychologists are engaged in the practice of both _____ science   pure

and _____ science as they gather information that may   applied
help alleviate a variety of social problems, including the generation gap, the abuse of drugs, and the results of the population explosion and urban growth.

self-test

_____ 1. Psychology can best be described as the
   a. systematic study of observable behavior and its relationship to covert processes and to external events in the environment
   b. scientific approach to the processes of thinking
   c. introspective attempt to explain and describe behavior in terms of its physiological causes
   d. analysis of human behavior

_____ 2. Two overt behaviors are
   a. thinking and remembering
   b. running and imagining
   c. thinking and writing the correct response to this item

   d. raising one's hand and responding in class

_____ 3. The goals of psychology are to
   a. understand and experiment with behavior
   b. conduct controlled experiments and use the scientific method
   c. understand and predict behavior
   d. control and manipulate human behavior

_____ 4. The statement that psychology is empirical means
   a. psychology is different from other sciences
   b. the methods of psychology are based on controlled experiments

and on observations made with the greatest possible precision and objectivity

   c. scientific psychology originated in the Greek and Roman ages

   d. psychological principles are based on the consensus of scientists

5. Each of the following phrases is most characteristic of the interests of Wundt, Galton, James, or Watson. Indicate your choice by writing the appropriate man's name in the space provided:

_____individual differences

_____behaviorism

_____first experimental laboratory

_____observable behavior

_____first systematic method of study

_____the contents of consciousness

_____differences in physical characteristics and mental abilities

_____"the achievement of the will"

_____mental life

_____heredity

_____human goals

_____ 6. The first psychology laboratory was
   a. devoted to the study of learning
   b. founded at Cornell
   c. founded over two hundred years ago
   d. established in 1879 in Leipzig

_____ 7. James might agree most with the proposition that
   a. humans are thinking organisms with ambitions and spiritual goals
   b. psychological facts should not be based on observations
   c. thinking can be observed as small throat movements made during thought
   d. the "will" cannot be studied

_____ 8. Between the time of James and the time of Watson psychologists grew dissatisfied with
   a. the scientific method
   b. introspection as a method of study
   c. sensation and perception as objects of study
   d. individual differences as a fruitful concern of psychology

_____ 9. The greatest disadvantage of the conception of psychology held by behaviorists was that it
   a. was nonscientific
   b. excluded many subject areas that rightly belong in psychology
   c. relied heavily on the subjective impression of the observer
   d. did not permit the study of individual differences

_____ 10. Which one of the following men is most closely associated with stimulus-response psychology?
   a. Rogers
   b. Skinner
   c. Wundt
   d. Maslow

_____ 11. A man associated with humanistic psychology is
   a. Maslow
   b. Piaget
   c. Kinsey
   d. James

_____ 12. In an experiment, one seeks to determine the influence of the
   a. independent variable on the dependent variable
   b. dependent variable on the independent variable
   c. independent variable on the behavior of the control group
   d. dependent variable on the behavior of the experimental group

_____ 13. In the single blind technique the
   a. experimenter does not know which group the subjects belong to

b. subjects do not know who the experimenter is

c. experimenter does not know the independent variable

d. subjects do not know which group they are in

_____14. In the double blind technique the
a. subjects and the experimenter do not know which group the subjects are in
b. subjects do not know the independent and dependent variables
c. experimenter does not know the independent and dependent variables
d. subjects and the experimenter do not know the independent and dependent variables

_____15. One of the primary requirements of naturalistic observation is to
a. control the situation
b. make the correct interpretations about why the observed behavior occurs prior to recording it
c. ensure that the observer is intimately acquainted with the causes of the behavior he is observing
d. minimize the effect of the presence of the observer on the situation being watched

_____16. A major difference between an experiment and a naturalistic observation is that one
a. is objective and the other is not
b. studies variables and the other does not
c. manipulates variables in the situation and the other does not
d. is scientific and the other is not

_____17. The major difference between an interview and a questionnaire concerns the
a. type of question asked
b. number of people who can be assessed in a short time
c. validity of an individual's response
d. amount of time required of the person being questioned

_____18. The largest group of applied psychologists are engaged in
a. industrial psychology
b. educational testing
c. vocational guidance
d. clinical psychology and counseling

_____19. Some psychologists believe the generation gap may essentially be caused by differences in
a. child-rearing practices
b. life styles
c. the percentage of young people receiving higher education
d. the willingness to talk about certain issues

_____20. Evidence from laboratory experiments suggests that the use of marijuana
a. makes people slightly more aggressive
b. prevents sleepiness
c. does not influence driving skill
d. affects short-term memory

Key to Self-Test

1. (a); 2. (d); 3. (c); 4. (b); 5. Galton, Watson, Wundt, Watson, Wundt, Wundt, Galton, James, James, Galton, James; 6. (d); 7. (a); 8. (b); 9. (b); 10. (b); 11. (a); 12. (a); 13. (d); 14. (a); 15. (d); 16. (c); 17. (b); 18. (d); 19. (c); 20. (d)

exercise

The preferred method of studying behavior is to conduct a scientific experiment. In psychology, a simple experiment might consist of randomly selecting two groups of subjects, then providing one group but not the other with a certain kind of experience. For example, suppose one wants to discover whether adult animals will learn a simple task better if they were raised in cages with a number of objects to explore than if they did not grow up exposed to these special stimuli. One might perform an experiment by randomly selecting two groups of twenty young rats and raising them in cages identical in every respect except that the cage for one group has several objects in it whereas the other cage is bare. When the rats have grown to adulthood they are tested on a simple learning task. If the group with the "enriched" experience of exploring the objects performs better than the other group, one can conclude that the presence of the objects was the cause, since the presence or absence of these stimuli was the only difference between the two groups.

As this example illustrates, the logic of the experimental method is basically simple. In practice, however, designing experiments that permit the researcher to draw unambiguous conclusions is actually quite an art. One of the most difficult aspects of designing precise experiments is to ensure that one and only one factor could possibly produce any observed difference in behavior.

To illustrate this point, consider the case of the logical alcoholic. Every night the alcoholic would go out and get drunk and the next morning he would be fogged in with a terrible hangover. He decided to conduct a "scientific experiment" to determine the cause of his hangover. The next night he drank bourbon and soda, and the following morning he had a terrible hangover. The following evening he changed to Scotch and soda, but again he was hung over in the morning. On the third evening of his "experiment" he drank gin and soda, and this again was followed by a morning-after hangover. The "researcher" concluded that liquor was obviously not the cause of his problem because he had had a different kind every night. It must have been the soda—for this was the only thing common to each type of drink.

This absurd example shows how easy it is to reach the false conclusion that one has isolated the single factor that produces a certain behavior. Below you will find descriptions of a few hypothetical experiments or conclusions. Write a short discussion of each, pointing out the adequacies and inadequacies of each experiment. Your major task should be to try to suggest factors other than the one mentioned that might have produced the results. There may be more than one way to view each situation.

1. A professor at Harvard wanted to know if college students could define a series of difficult vocabulary words that were to appear in a textbook he was writing. Since it turned out that his own students could correctly define an average of 90 percent of the words, he concluded that most college students would have no trouble with the vocabulary in his new text.

2. A survey of 2000 married couples showed that only one-third as many divorces occurred among couples in which both members had graduated from college as among couples in which neither member had graduated. Therefore, a college education improves the stability of marriages.

3. Autopsies of schizophrenic patients at a mental hospital showed that the schizophrenics had much larger adrenal glands than a group of normal people. (The adrenal glands secrete substances into the blood that provide one with emergency energy when confronted with dangerous or anxious situations.) The researcher concluded that having large adrenal glands causes schizophrenia.

4. A group of 1000 men who smoked at least two packs of cigarettes a day and another group of 1000 men who did not smoke at all were selected so that for every man in one group there was a man in the other of the same age, height, weight, intelligence, and income. After twenty years of observation there were three times as many deaths attributed to lung cancer among the smokers as among the nonsmokers. Therefore, smoking causes lung cancer.

5. A psychologist wanted to know if marijuana really produces a "high." He randomly selected a number of college students and assigned them either to an experimental group or to a control group. The experimental group was given some marijuana to smoke; the control group smoked ordinary cigarettes. Later the students wrote a description of their feelings after smoking, and the experimenter rated the descriptions for their degree of unusual content. The results showed that the marijuana group had much higher ratings for unusual content. The psychologist concluded that marijuana did produce a type of "high."

CHAPTER 2

THE PRINCIPLES OF LEARNING

programed unit

1. Much of the behavior of lower organisms is regulated by *instincts*, which are elaborate inborn patterns of activity. A bird building a nest and a spider spinning a web are acting according to _____.

   instincts

2. An important part of the definition of instinct is that the behavior is *inborn*. This means that the organism will exhibit the behavior without prior learning. Since salmon migrate from their birthplace in a river to the ocean and back again without being taught, this migration is an _____ pattern of behavior, called an _____.

   inborn, instinct

3. Most human behavior depends not on instincts but on learning. For example, humans learn to build many kinds of houses and to raise their children in many different ways, whereas in lower organisms these behaviors are largely regulated by _____.

   instincts

4. The *reflex*, which is a brief automatic response to a fairly specific stimulus, is an inborn behavior displayed by humans and lower organisms. The eyeblink, in response to the stimulus of an object approaching the eye, is a common _____.

   reflex

5. The difference between an instinct and a reflex rests in the elaborateness of the response. A brief automatic response to a fairly specific stimulus is a _____, but a more intricate inborn pattern of activity constitutes an _____.

   reflex

   instinct

6. If you stroke a baby's cheek at the left side of his mouth, he will turn his head to the left. This automatic reaction to stroking the cheek is another example of a _____.

   reflex

7. Every reflex is a response to a *stimulus*, which can be defined as any

form of energy capable of exciting the nervous system. In the example above, the stroke of the baby's cheek acted as the _____   stimulus for the head turn.

8. *Review*

    a. Elaborate inborn patterns of behavior are _____.   instincts

    b. A brief automatic response to a fairly specific stimulus is a _____.   reflex

    c. Any form of energy capable of exciting the nervous system consti-

       tutes a _____.   stimulus

9. *Pavlov,* a Russian scientist, was interested in the possible learned relationship between a stimulus and a reflex. Specifically, he knew that a reflex was evoked by the occurrence of a specific stimulus. Through learning, could this reflex be made to occur to stimuli that ordinarily did not evoke it? The possibility of a learned reflex response was the

    primary concern of _____.   Pavlov

10. Pavlov used the term *conditioning* to imply this type of learning. The process of learning to associate a reflex with a new stimulus is referred

     to as _____.   conditioning

11. Forms of the term conditioning are used to refer to the reflex and its stimulus. An unlearned reflex to a specific stimulus is termed the *unconditioned response.* Salivating when food is placed in the mouth or blinking one's eye when a strong puff of air is directed on it are both

    examples of an _____ _____.   unconditioned response

12. The stimulus that automatically elicits an unconditioned response is called an *unconditioned stimulus.* In the illustrations in frame 11 above,

    the food and the puff of air are examples of an _____   unconditioned

    _____.   stimulus

13. When a child touches a hot stove, the heat of the stove acts as an

    _____ _____ for the sudden   unconditioned stimulus

    withdrawal of his hand. Removal of the hand is the _____   unconditioned

    _____.   response

14. Pavlov's famous experiment consisted of sounding a metronome just before placing food in a dog's mouth. In technical terminology, a metro-

    nome was sounded just prior to presenting the _____   unconditioned

    _____ of food, which produced the _____   stimulus, unconditioned

    _____ of salivation.   response

15. Pavlov wanted to know if through the frequent pairing of the sound

of the metronome with the presentation of food the dog would learn to salivate to the metronome alone, without having food present. Pavlov was investigating the process of learning to associate a reflex with a neutral stimulus—one that ordinarily had no effect on the dog. This

learning process is called _____.   conditioning

16. Since the dog did learn, or was conditioned, to salivate to the sound of the metronome, salivating to the metronome was the *conditioned response*. A reflex that has become associated with a new stimulus through

learning is a _____ _____.   conditioned response

17. If a tone was sounded just before a puff of air produced the reflex of blinking, the blink might become conditioned to occur when the tone was presented alone. A blink occurring to the tone would then be a

_____ _____.   conditioned response

18. Notice that the difference between an unconditioned and a conditioned response resides mainly in the nature of the stimulus that precedes it. If the presence of food (unconditioned stimulus) elicits salivation, the

salivation is called an _____ _____.   unconditioned response
However, if the previously neutral stimulus of the metronome elicits

salivation, the salivation is a _____ _____.   conditioned response

19. The stimulus that through conditioning elicits the conditioned response is called the *conditioned stimulus*. In the case of Pavlov's experiment,

the metronome was the _____ _____.   conditioned stimulus

20. In the tone-puff-blink situation, the tone is the previously neutral stimulus that through conditioning comes to elicit the blink and is there-

fore the _____ _____.   conditioned stimulus

21. *Review*
   a. The famous pioneer who discovered that reflexes could be modified

   by learning was _____. The learning process he investi-   Pavlov

   gated is called _____.   conditioning
   b. Pavlov's experiment involved repeatedly sounding a metronome just before placing food in a dog's mouth. The food was the natural stimulus for salivation, but the dog soon learned to salivate to the sound of the metronome without the presentation of food. In this

   experiment, the food, called the _____   unconditioned

   _____, invariably produced the _____   stimulus, unconditioned

   _____ of salivation.   response

   c. Ultimately, the salivation was conditioned to occur to the _____   conditioned

_____ of the metronome. When that happened the   stimulus

salivation became the _____ _____.   conditioned response

22. This simple experiment illustrates a learning process known as *classical conditioning*. The association of a response with a previously neutral stimulus by repeatedly pairing an unconditioned stimulus with a conditioned stimulus is called _____ _____.   classical conditioning

23. The experiment of the Russian scientist _____ illustrates   Pavlov
the learning process of _____ _____.   classical conditioning

24. In classical conditioning, the pairing of the unconditioned stimulus with a conditioned stimulus is called *reinforcement*. The pairing of food with the sound of the metronome constitutes _____.   reinforcement

25. The term *reinforcement* is used because the food establishes and strengthens, or "reinforces," the association between metronome and salivation. Therefore, the pairing of an unconditioned stimulus with a conditioned stimulus is called _____.   reinforcement

26. In the example involving the eyeblink, the puff of air is the unconditioned stimulus, and the tone-puff pairing constitutes _____.   reinforcement

27. Reinforcement is so vital to classical conditioning that if it is discontinued, the conditioned response gradually subsides until it eventually disappears, a phenomenon known as *extinction*. For example, if the metronome is no longer followed by food, the dog will eventually cease to salivate to the sound of the metronome. When that happens, psychologists say the conditioned response has undergone _____.   extinction

28. The gradual disappearance of the conditioned response as a result of discontinuing reinforcement (that is, omitting the unconditioned stimulus) constitutes _____.   extinction

29. If the puff of air is later omitted from the tone-puff pairing, the conditioned response of blinking to the tone will undergo _____.   extinction

30. However, suppose that a period of rest is introduced after the conditioned response is extinguished and no longer occurs. When the conditioned stimulus is next presented after the rest, the conditioned response may occur again. This is known as *spontaneous recovery*. If a rest is introduced after extinction in Pavlov's experiment, the next presentation of the metronome might again elicit the conditioned response of salivation without additional reinforcements. This would constitute _____ _____.   spontaneous recovery

31. The recurrence of the conditioned response after extinction and rest

    is known as _____ _____.   spontaneous recovery

32. Pavlov used a metronome as the conditioned stimulus in his experiment. Suppose a dog was classically conditioned in the Pavlovian manner and then a buzzer rather than the metronome was suddenly substituted as the conditioned stimulus and food was no longer presented. If the dog also salivates to the buzzer, such behavior would be called *stimulus generalization*. The occurrence of a learned response to a stimulus that

    is similar to the original conditioned stimulus is called _____   stimulus

    _____.   generalization

33. Apparently the dog "generalizes" its response of salivation from one stimulus to another — that is, from the metronome to the buzzer. When a response has been conditioned to one stimulus, it is also likely to occur

    to similar stimuli through the process of _____   stimulus

    _____.   generalization

34. Through further training the organism can be taught to respond only to one stimulus and not to others. This phenomenon is known as *stimulus discrimination*. If a bell is always followed by an air puff but a buzzer is not, the subject soon learns to blink only to the sound of the bell and

    not to the buzzer through the process of _____   stimulus

    _____.   discrimination

35. The crucial factor in producing stimulus discrimination is selective reinforcement. Notice in the example in frame 34 above that the bell is followed by the reinforcement of the air puff and the buzzer is not.

    The result of such selective reinforcement is _____   stimulus

    _____.   discrimination

36. *Review*

    a. The learning process by which a response becomes associated with a previously neutral stimulus by repeatedly pairing an unconditioned

       stimulus with a conditioned stimulus is called _____   classical

       _____.   conditioning

    b. The pairing of the unconditioned stimulus with the conditioned

       stimulus constitutes _____. However,   reinforcement
       when reinforcement is omitted, the conditioned response undergoes

       _____. If a rest is then introduced, the condi-   extinction
       tioned response may reappear on the next presentation of the con-

       ditioned stimulus — a phenomenon called _____ _____.   spontaneous recovery

c. The occurrence of a conditioned response to stimuli that are similar to the original conditioned stimulus is known as _____ _____. Through further training the conditioned response can be made to occur only to one stimulus and not to others—a process known as _____ _____.

stimulus
generalization

stimulus
discrimination

37. Another important form of behavior in the study of learning is called *operant behavior.* Operant behavior is the seemingly random, spontaneous activity initiated by the organism, with which it appears to "operate" on the environment. When a rat is placed in a strange cage, it may explore, sniff, and climb about. This activity constitutes _____ _____.

operant behavior

38. Through learning, operant behavior can become attached to a specific stimulus. This process is called *operant conditioning* to distinguish it from classical conditioning. In operant conditioning the organism learns to repeat one component of its operant behavior when presented with certain stimuli. For example, if a rat learns to press a bar that produces a food reward, psychologists say _____ _____ has occurred.

operant
conditioning

39. In the example in frame 38 above, the food establishes and maintains the response of bar pressing. Therefore, it constitutes a reinforcement. In this context, a reinforcement is a stimulus following a behavior that induces repetitions of that behavior. Following a bar press with food induces more bar pressing. Therefore, food is a _____.

reinforcement

40. In both Pavlov's experiment and in learning to bar press, food establishes and maintains a response and is therefore a _____ in these situations.

reinforcement

41. One of the fundamental differences between classical and operant conditioning is the fact that in one case the experimenter can produce the desired response at his will whereas in the other he must wait until the animal makes the behavior on its own before he can reinforce it. The experimenter can control when the desired response occurs in _____ conditioning, but initially the organism determines its occurrence in _____ conditioning.

classical

operant

42. Since operant conditioning is dependent on the organism's performing the desired response, there needs to be some way to learn new responses

that would not occur spontaneously. One method is by *shaping* behavior. The learning of unique responses through operant conditioning is called

_____.   shaping

43. *Shaping* involves the reinforcement of responses that progressively approximate the form of the desired behavior. For example, to get a pigeon to peck a black dot inside a white circle one might first reward the pigeon with food for merely facing the circle. Later, when this is learned, reward might be given the bird for approaching the circle and then touching it with its beak. Finally, the pigeon must peck the black dot in order to receive reward. Thus the desired behavior is gradually

developed through the process of _____.   shaping

44. Just as *extinction, spontaneous recovery, stimulus generalization,* and *stimulus discrimination* operate in classical conditioning, they can also take place in operant conditioning. The cessation of reinforcement

leads to _____, but with a rest _____   extinction, spontaneous

_____ may occur.   recovery

45. The occurrence of the learned operant response in a stimulus context that is similar but not identical with that present during the original

learning constitutes _____ _____,   stimulus generalization
and learning to perform the response to one stimulus but not to similar

stimuli illustrates _____ _____.   stimulus discrimination

46. *Learning through observation* is another kind of learning process. The organism learns by observing and imitating the behavior of others. "Monkey see, monkey do" is a popular adage that refers to learning

through _____.   observation

47. In one experiment, two cats learned to obtain food by pressing a bar when a light went on. Then other cats were permitted to observe them obtain food in this manner. The cats that watched the trained animals were then tested, and they learned the bar-pressing task much more quickly than animals not allowed to watch. Apparently, they learned

through _____.   observation

48. *Review*
   a. The process of learning to attach some spontaneously occurring

   behavior (known as _____ behavior) to a specific   operant

   stimulus is called _____ _____.   operant conditioning
   b. The stimulus (for example, food) that establishes and maintains the

   learned behavior is called a _____.   reinforcement
   c. An essential difference between classical and operant conditioning

resides in the fact that the desired behavior can be elicited by a

specific stimulus at the beginning of _____   classical

_____ whereas one must wait for the de-   conditioning

sired behavior to occur spontaneously in _____   operant

_____.   conditioning

d. The learning of new or complex behavior through operant conditioning of responses that gradually approximate the desired

behavior is called _____.   shaping

e. One often learns new behavior by watching and imitating the be-

havior of someone else; this is learning through _____.   observation

49. In all forms of learning, just what is learned is something of a mystery.
The more or less permanent change that occurs within the nervous
system during learning is best described as a *mediational unit*. What

is actually learned is a _____ _____.   mediational unit

50. A mediational unit is difficult to define. A good approximation is that
it is some sort of more or less permanent nerve pathway or pattern
established inside the organism through learning. It serves as an inter-
mediary between a stimulus and an immediate or future behavior or
mental activity. That is, an associative bridge between a stimulus and

a response is a _____ _____.   mediational unit

51. Words, concepts, attitudes, motives, and emotions are all learned
associations between stimuli and responses and therefore may serve

as _____ _____.   mediational units

52. A key aspect of the learning situation is reinforcement. A reinforcement such as food derives its power from the fact that it satisfies a
basic need of the organism. Food is an example of a *primary reinforcing
stimulus*. A stimulus that is itself rewarding to the organism consti-

tutes a _____ _____ _____.   primary reinforcing
stimulus

53. But some stimuli come to have the power of reinforcement through
a learned association with a primary reinforcing stimulus. Such a stimulus is called a *secondary reinforcing stimulus*. If a mother feeds and
fondles her infant, the mere presence of the mother may then reward

behavior as a _____ _____   secondary reinforcing

_____.   stimulus

54. Reinforcement may be given every time the organism performs the
desired response, or it may be given only sometimes. Reward given on
only some but not all occasions when the animal responds with the
appropriate behavior is known as *partial reinforcement*. If a rat is re-

warded for every other bar press or for the first press in each consecutive minute, the rat is said to be learning under _____ _____.

partial

reinforcement

55. When reinforcement is withdrawn, behavior learned under partial reinforcement tends to be more persistent than behavior rewarded on every trial. Psychologists say that responses "resist extinction" to a greater extent if they were learned under _____ _____ than if reinforcement was given each time the correct response occurred.

partial

reinforcement

56. Learning that takes place but is not displayed in the organism's performance until reinforcement is provided is called *latent learning*. If a rat is allowed to explore a maze without any reinforcement at all, later when reward is given, the animal's performance is better than if such exploration had not been allowed. Apparently, the "familiarization" period permitted _____ _____ to occur.

latent learning

57. *Review*

a. It is likely that what is learned in most situations is an associative bridge between a stimulus and a response, called a _____ _____.

mediational

unit

b. A stimulus that is rewarding in itself is called a _____ reinforcing stimulus.

primary

c. A stimulus that has become rewarding through association with a primary reinforcing stimulus may be used as a _____ reinforcing stimulus.

secondary

d. Reinforcement that is presented only after some appropriate responses, not after every one, is known as _____ _____.

partial

reinforcement

e. Learning that takes place but is not reflected in overt performance until after reinforcement is provided constitutes _____ _____.

latent

learning

self-test

_____ 1. An instinct is a(n)
   a. learned behavior
   b. brief automatic response to a fairly specific stimulus
   c. elaborate inborn behavior pattern
   d. behavior pattern that develops over the life span of the organism

_____ 2. The question of whether intelligence is primarily fixed at birth or is a product of one's experience is
   a. largely settled by modern psychology
   b. a problem for the developers of the I.Q. test
   c. the concern of philosophy, not psychology
   d. an example of the "nature versus nurture" issue

_____ 3. The concept of the *tabula rasa* has been used to suggest that
   a. not very much is learned in the early months of life
   b. most human behavior is determined by experience and learning
   c. lower animals learn more than they inherit
   d. heredity predisposes us to certain behavior

_____ 4. The distinction between an instinct and a reflex centers around the
   a. survival value of the behavior
   b. inborn versus learned nature of the behavior
   c. elaborateness of the behavior
   d. amount of thinking required to plan and execute the behavior

_____ 5. A reflex is a(n)
   a. brief learned response to a specific stimulus
   b. behavior that is more characteristic of humans than of lower organisms
   c. relatively simple and specific inborn response to a given stimulus
   d. elaborate inborn pattern of behavior

_____ 6. The kind of learning that Pavlov studied is called
   a. operant conditioning
   b. instinctive learning
   c. reflexology
   d. classical conditioning

7. In Pavlov's experiment there [are] kinds of stimuli and responses, all o[f] have special names. Write the names i[n] space provided.

_____salivation to the metronome

_____the metronome

_____the food

_____salivation to the food

8. Apply the same technical terminology that Pavlov used to the following aspects of the "Albert experiment."

_____fear response to the loud noise

_____fear response to the sight of the rat

_____the rat

_____the loud noise

_____ 9. In classical conditioning the conditioned stimulus is usually
   a. a sound
   b. made by the organism
   c. presented before the unconditioned stimulus
   d. food or water

_____10. A type of learning not *initially* dependent on a stimulus that produces a specific response is called
   a. operant conditioning
   b. reflex learning
   c. discrimination learning
   d. classical conditioning

_____11. Stimulus discrimination and generalization
   a. are both needed to explain why Albert was afraid of the rabbit after learning to be afraid in the presence of the rat
   b. usually do not play a significant role in adult human behavior
   c. occur only as a function of imitation

...ior learned by op-
...s classical condition-

...primarily related to operant
...oning and not to classical condi-
...oning is
a. reinforcement
b. shaping
c. spontaneous recovery
d. stimulus generalization

_____13. Which one of the following bodily
activities *cannot* be altered by classical
or operant conditioning?
a. heart rate
b. intestinal contractions
c. blood pressure
d. all of these can be modified by
conditioning

_____14. An association established by learning
may be called a(n)
a. instinct
b. free operant
c. mediational unit
d. reflex

_____15. Stimuli that effectively reinforce a
given human response
a. tend to alter the frequency and
strength of that response
b. tend to be the same from person
to person
c. usually reduce a biological need
d. usually are regarded as pleasant

_____16. A neutral stimulus can become a
secondary reinforcing stimulus as a
result of
a. classical conditioning
b. its capacity to satisfy biological
drives
c. association with operant behavior
d. stimulus discrimination

_____17. Ordinarily, operant conditioning will
occur most rapidly if the reinforcement is

a. small and immediately follows the
desired response
b. substantial and immediately follows the desired response
c. small and occurs several seconds
after the desired response
d. substantial and occurs several
seconds after the desired response

_____18. Partial reinforcement, as opposed to
constant reinforcement, produces
a. faster learning
b. slower extinction
c. more rapid shaping
d. less spontaneous recovery

_____19. Latent learning is learning that is
manifested in overt performance
a. only after reinforcement is introduced
b. only after a moderately long delay
of reinforcement
c. during spontaneous recovery
d. during unrewarded trials

_____20. The phenomenon of latent learning
attests to the fact that
a. food is not the only primary reinforcing stimulus
b. animals like to work for a reward
even if it is provided after a delay
c. learning sometimes occurs several
days after the training session
d. learning may occur without obvious primary or secondary reinforcement

Key to Self-Test

1. (c); 2. (d); 3. (b); 4. (c); 5. (c); 6. (d);
7. conditioned response, conditioned stimulus,
unconditioned stimulus, unconditioned response;
8. unconditioned response, conditioned response,
conditioned stimulus, unconditioned stimulus;
9. (c); 10. (a); 11. (d); 12. (b); 13. (d); 14.
(c); 15. (a); 16. (a); 17. (b); 18. (b); 19.
(a); 20. (d)

exercises

I. Consider the following description of a learning situation outside the laboratory:

A three-year-old girl had just moved into a new house with a big back yard enclosed by a white picket fence. Next door, there was a large white dog. Every time the little girl would go near the fence on that side of her yard, the dog would jump against the fence and bark at her. Fortunately, the people on the other side of the house owned a friendly small black poodle that soon became one of the girl's best friends. Years later, the girl was still afraid of large white dogs but not of small dark-colored ones. Further, she was reluctant to pet and hold the white rabbits in her biology classroom, but she adored brown hamsters.

Questions

1. Describe the learning in this case by identifying the unconditioned stimulus and response and the conditioned stimulus and response.
2. How do you explain the fact that the girl was afraid only of some dogs? What is this kind of learning called?
3. How do you explain the fact that she was apprehensive about some animals in her biology class and not about others? What is this called?

II. Suppose a researcher was interested in teaching myna birds to vocalize. Two small groups of birds were given a daily training session, *after* which they were fed. Since the birds were hungry, the experimenter would give them a food grain if they vocalized during the training period. The two groups of birds were treated somewhat differently, however. One group (group A) received a food grain after *every* vocalization whereas the other group (group B) was fed only after every *third* vocalization. This training was continued for 30 days and then followed by 30 days during which no food was given for vocalizations. The average number of vocalizations per day is plotted for the two groups in Figure 2–1.

Questions

1. What is this kind of learning called?
2. In what ways does it differ from the kind of learning described in the preceding exercise?
3. What learning term is applied to the food in this example?
4. The two groups in the experiment have different schedules of reward. What kind of reinforcement does group B receive?

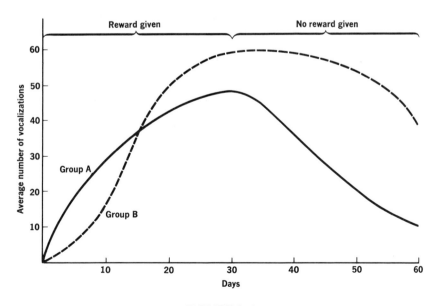

FIGURE 2–1

5. Notice in Figure 2–1 that group B starts slower and finishes better. Can you offer a possible explanation for this?

6. What is the performance during days 30–60 called?

7. Group B tends to respond with more vocalizations than group A when neither group is being rewarded. Is this an unusual result under these circumstances? Cite examples from the text that might have led you to predict such an outcome.

CHAPTER 3 REMEMBERING AND FORGETTING

programed unit

1. If one plots on a graph the amount of material remembered for different lengths of time after an initial learning attempt, one has drawn a *curve of forgetting.* Ebbinghaus was the first man to study forgetting systematically, and he charted its course in a _____ _____ _____.

   curve of forgetting

2. Ebbinghaus found that when we learn something new, we quickly forget much of what we have learned, but we remember at least some of it for a long time. Therefore, a curve showing a rapid drop followed by a leveling off would represent a typical _____ _____ _____.

   curve of forgetting

3. There are three principal ways of measuring learning. The first is to ask a person to *recall* the material he has learned. When a teacher gives an essay test, he measures learning by the method of _____.

   recall

4. Another method is to test *recognition.* A multiple-choice or true-false examination measures learning by testing _____.

   recognition

5. Recall tends to be more difficult than recognition. For example, if a student did not study much for a history quiz, he might be able to pick out the correct answer from among several choices, but he would have a harder time constructing a detailed essay in which he must produce the facts himself. Consequently, a poorly prepared student might prefer to be tested by the method of _____ rather than

   recognition

   by that of _____.

   recall

6. A third method of measuring learning is *relearning.* Ebbinghaus learned his material and later relearned it. Usually it took him fewer trials to

learn it the second time than the first, and the number of such trials

"saved" was Ebbinghaus's measure of _____ .   relearning

7. Actually, these measures of learning usually reflect more than just learning or forgetting—they also reflect *performance*. Often a young child who is learning to talk will say "Mama" or "Dada" endlessly at home but will not utter a sound when asked to perform for strangers. Certainly, his failure to say "Dada" is a failure not of learning but of

_____ .   performance

8. *Review*
   a. Ebbinghaus's study of forgetting resulted in a typical _____   curve

   ____ _____ .   of forgetting

   b. Three principal ways of measuring learning are _____ ,   recall

   _____ , and _____ .   recognition, relearning

   c. These measures of learning actually reflect not only learning or

   forgetting but also _____ .   performance

9. There are several theories of why we forget. One of the oldest theories described forgetting as the *fading of the memory trace*. According to this theory, a memory is like a path through a field—it fades with time unless it is continuously used. However, some people remember things for remarkable lengths of time without additional practice. Conse-

   quently, forgetting is probably not simply a _____ of the   fading

   _____ _____ .   memory trace

10. A second theory of forgetting focused on the *distortion of the memory trace*. This theory was based on the observation that major themes of complex material are usually remembered, but the details are often forgotten. In trying to reconstruct these missing details, we frequently distort them. Remembering the plot of a story but changing the names

    of the characters illustrates the _____ of the   distortion

    _____ _____ .   memory trace

11. Two historically interesting theories of forgetting focused on the memory trace. The suggestion that a memory as a whole became less clear

    with time was known as the _____ of the memory trace,   fading
    while memory for major themes but misrepresentation of details was

    known as the _____ of the memory trace.   distortion

12. A third theory of forgetting suggests that we often forget simply because we want to forget. This is the theory of *motivated forgetting*. People

who gamble tend to remember their winning moments but forget their

losses. They display _____ _____.   motivated forgetting

13. The psychoanalytic theory of repression, in which unpleasant memories are thought to be pushed into the unconscious, is closely related to the

theory of _____ _____.   motivated forgetting

14. A fourth theory of forgetting centers around the word *interference*. It holds that when we learn something, our ability to remember it is interfered with by things we have learned previously and also by things we learn in the future. When our memory of some material is disturbed

by other learning, psychologists say _____   interference
has occurred.

15. Confusing the names of two people or blurting out a Spanish phrase when

trying to speak French illustrates the concept of _____.   interference

16. Much of the evidence for this theory derives from research on two specific types of interference. One type, called *retroactive inhibition*, occurs if the learning of task 2 interferes with the memory of previously learned task 1. Frequently, if a student learns French and then German, the retention of the French suffers because German was studied later.

That is, remembering French comes under the influence of _____   retroactive

_____.   inhibition

17. This type of interference is called retroactive inhibition because the learning of task 2 seems to "act back" to interfere with the memory of task 1. Thus, the partial or complete blocking out of old memories by

new learning constitutes _____ _____.   retroactive inhibition

18. The ability to remember new material may be reduced by something learned in the past. This type of interference is called *proactive inhibition*. Often when initially attempting to learn a second foreign language, words from the previously learned language keep slipping into one's speech. If a student learns Spanish and then French, in the initial attempts to speak French he may blurt out the Spanish word instead of

the intended French word because of _____   proactive

_____.   inhibition

19. Although both retroactive and proactive inhibition involve interference with the memory of a task, they differ with respect to the direction of that influence. If previously learned task 1 is difficult to remember

because of subsequently learning task 2, _____   retroactive

_____ has occurred. Conversely, if task 2 is diffi-   inhibition cult to remember because of previously learned task 1, _____   proactive

_____ has occurred.   inhibition

20. Finally, a fifth theory characterizes forgetting as a *failure in retrieval*. This approach suggests that the key process in forgetting may not be a failure in the learning or retention of information but rather an inability to bring forth the appropriate memories from storage. Such an

inability is termed a _____ ____ _____.   failure in retrieval

21. When a certain area of the brain is electrically stimulated during brain surgery, subjects are able to remember many details about events from their distant past that they could not recall at all without brain stimulation. Apparently the memories are "in storage," but they cannot ordi-

narily be recalled because of some _____ _____   failure in

_____.   retrieval

22. *Review*
    a. Two theories of forgetting center on the term _____   memory

    _____. One theory emphasizes the weakening of a memory   trace

    for an entire event, or the _____ of the memory trace.   fading
    Remembering major themes but changing some of the details de-

    scribes the theory of the _____ of the memory   distortion
    trace.
    b. Forgetting what we want to forget characterizes the theory of

    _____ _____.   motivated forgetting
    c. A fourth theory of forgetting focuses on the fact that memories for
    one task may be disturbed by other learning, a process known as

    _____.   interference
    d. When memories for one task are interfered with by previous learn-

    ing, _____ _____ has   proactive inhibition
    occurred. When memories for one task are interfered with by subse-

    quent learning, _____ _____   retroactive inhibition
    has occurred.
    e. A fifth theory characterizes forgetting as an inability to bring forth

    the appropriate memories from storage, that is, as a _____   failure

    ____ _____.   in retrieval

23. There are apparently three kinds of memory systems. The first is *sensory memory,* which contains the briefly lingering traces of information sent to the brain by the senses. The short-lived image of a telephone number that remains in one's mind after closing the telephone book

reflects the operation of the _____ _____ system.   sensory memory

24. Ordinarily, information in the first memory system, _____   sensory

    _____, is lost within a few tenths of a second.   memory

25. However, information is often transferred to the second system, *short-term memory*. Information stored in short-term memory is retained somewhat longer than in sensory memory, perhaps up to thirty seconds. A phone number remembered long enough to dial it is an example of

    material kept in _____-_____ _____.   short-term memory

26. A supermarket cashier remembers only briefly that she must give a customer $5.28 change from a twenty-dollar bill; by the time she begins checking out the next customer, the figure $5.28 has already been lost

    from her _____-_____ _____.   short-term memory

27. One of the several kinds of processes that probably characterize short-term memory is *scanning* of the information in sensory memory. Presumably, the transfer of material from sensory to short-term memory is

    aided by this _____ process.   scanning

28. In addition, there is likely some sort of *rehearsal system* to keep material active in short-term memory. We often keep saying a telephone number to ourselves until we have dialed it completely. This behavior pre-

    sumably reflects some kind of _____ _____.   rehearsal system

29. The activity of the short-term memory system involves surveying the

    sensory memory system by _____ and "practicing"   scanning

    material through some type of _____ _____.   rehearsal system

30. Material not lost from short-term memory may be transferred to the third memory system, *long-term memory,* which is the permanent storehouse of information. For instance, one's own name and birth date

    would be stored in _____-_____ _____.   long-term memory

31. Though some memories may be destroyed through brain injury or loss of brain cells with aging, most students of memory believe that

    once stored, most memories are retained permanently in _____-   long-

    _____ _____.   term memory

32. *Review*
    a. The memory system containing the lingering traces of information

       sent to the brain by the senses is the _____   sensory

       _____ system.   memory

    b. Sensory information is often transferred to the second system,

_____-_____ _____, which reviews the   short-term memory

sensory memory by _____ and keeps memories alive   scanning

through some type of _____ _____.   rehearsal system

c. The permanent storehouse of information is the _____-   long-

_____ _____ system.   term memory

33. Material is transferred from short-term to long-term memory through some *coding* process. This process involves relating the new information to mediational units already in long-term memory. A telephone number (621–1940) that is recognized as being one's birth date (6/21/1940) would be quickly entered into long-term memory. Relating the number

to the existing memory of one's birth date characterizes the _____   coding
process.

34. Associating new information with mediational units already in long-

term memory characterizes the _____ process, whereby   coding
new material is transferred to long-term memory.

35. The process of extracting information from long-term memory is called *retrieval*. Many psychologists believe that long-term memory constitutes a permanent storehouse of information and that nothing is lost from this system; forgetting is conceived to be merely a failure in

_____.   retrieval

36. One strategy that facilitates the coding and retrieval processes is *making up stories* to integrate diverse material. In an experiment some students were asked to memorize a list of random words by devising a narrative incorporating them, while others simply memorized the words. Those

who learned through the technique of _____ _____   making up

_____ remembered the material better.   stories

37. Another technique is to learn by *categories*. For example, if in a long list of words to be learned "horse, aardvark, mole" are grouped under the label "animal," remembering the concept of animal will help recall the three species. Here coding and retrieval are aided through learning

by _____.   categories

38. *Review*
   a. Material is transferred to long-term memory through some _____ coding
      process.
   b. The process of extracting information from long-term memory is

   called _____.   retrieval

   c. Two strategies that facilitate coding and retrieval are _____   making

_____ _____and learning by _____.   up stories, categories

39. There are at least three basic requirements for learning. The first is a *distinctive stimulus*. If a person is to remember a given stimulus or relate it to other stimuli or actions, that stimulus must stand out. It must

be _____.   distinctive

40. A lecturer who speaks in a monotone does not emphasize his points, and therefore learning from him is difficult because he does not pro-

vide _____ stimuli.   distinctive

41. It is not sufficient merely to have a distinctive stimulus; the learner must pay *attention* to it. Obviously, the dozing student is incapable of

learning much from a lecture because he is not paying _____   attention
to the relevant stimuli.

42. These two requirements for learning frequently work together. A

monotonous lecturer failing to provide _____   distinctive
stimuli to highlight important points is likely to be so boring that

students cannot maintain their _____to his discourse.   attention

43. The third requirement for learning is some kind of unit within the organism to which the stimulus can be *attached*. Pavlov's dog could not have learned to salivate to the sound of the metronome if it did not have the capacity to make the response of salivation. In this case, the capacity to salivate was the unit to which the stimulus of the metronome

could be _____.   attached

44. The unit to which a stimulus may become attached may be *innate* or previously *learned*. The capacity to salivate in the presence of food and

to blink one's eye when an object approaches it are _____   innate
attachment units. The knowledge of how to perform certain guitar chords that can later be integrated into a melody constitutes a previously

_____ attachment unit.   learned

45. Many attachment units do not involve direct links with overt behavior, but instead they are composed of covert mental processes. They are previously learned *mediational units*. For example, we have learned the English word *house*. Now suppose we study Spanish and are confronted with the word *casa*, which also means house. The word *casa* then becomes associated with all that we have previously learned about the English word *house*. In this case, a set of covert and previously learned

associations constitutes the _____ _____.   mediational unit

46. It follows that the more associations we possess prior to entering a learn-

ing situation, the more likely it is that we will meet the third require-

ment of learning, which is the possession of an _____ or   innate

previously _____ attachment unit with which a stimulus   learned
may become associated.

47. Review
  a. There are three basic requirements for learning. One requirement

      is a stimulus that stands out and is therefore _____.   distinctive

  b. The second requirement is that the learner pay _____   attention
      to the distinctive stimulus.
  c. The third requirement for learning is possession of a unit to which

      the stimulus can be _____. Attachment units that   attached
      do not involve direct links with overt behavior but are composed of

      covert mental processes are _____ units.   mediational

      Attachment units may be _____ or previously _____.   innate, learned

self-test

_____ 1. Ebbinghaus experimented with non-sense syllables rather than real words because they were
    a. harder to learn than words
    b. likely to be unique in a person's experience
    c. subtly related to meaningful words
    d. likely to be forgotten more easily

_____ 2. Ebbinghaus measured forgetting by
    a. testing how many of the syllables he could recall in a sitting
    b. recognizing the syllables he had learned in a long list of other syllables
    c. recording the difference between the time required to relearn a list of syllables and the time required to learn it originally
    d. noting how much interference the first list of syllables generated in learning a new list that was very similar to the original

_____ 3. The typical curve of forgetting indicates that we
    a. continue to forget substantial amounts of material long after original learning
    b. forget nearly everything within a very short time after learning
    c. do not forget much immediately after learning but forget rapidly thereafter
    d. forget most rapidly immediately after learning but do retain something for remarkably long periods of time

_____ 4. The distinction between learning and memory on the one hand and performance on the other implies that the curve of forgetting
    a. really reflects only performance and not learning or forgetting
    b. is useless in assessing learning and memory
    c. reflects a combination of learning, motivation, and performance
    d. reflects only forgetting and separate procedures are needed to assess performance ability

_____ 5. Multiple-choice questions test learning by the method of
   a. recall
   b. recognition
   c. relearning
   d. redintegration

_____ 6. The disadvantage of the method of relearning is that it
   a. cannot always be easily carried out
   b. does not reflect some types of memory
   c. is too easy
   d. works only for verbal material

_____ 7. The memory trace conception is probably not a sufficient explanation of memory and forgetting because
   a. there is no such thing as a memory trace
   b. sensory memory is much too short
   c. some experiences are permanently stored in memory even if they cannot be recalled under ordinary circumstances
   d. neurophysiological evidence indicates that the nervous system does not operate in this manner

_____ 8. The inability to remember an embarrassing moment may illustrate the concept of
   a. motivated forgetting
   b. retroactive inhibition
   c. proactive inhibition
   d. a decayed memory trace

_____ 9. Learning French after having learned Spanish may make Spanish harder to remember, illustrating the concept of
   a. retroactive inhibition
   b. a memory trace
   c. proactive inhibition
   d. motivated forgetting

_____ 10. Many psychologists believe that failure to remember something is basically a problem in
   a. retrieval
   b. learning
   c. chunking
   d. distinguishing stimuli

_____ 11. Rapid flow of information and forgetting within about thirty seconds are characteristic of
   a. sensory memory
   b. the sensory register
   c. long-term memory
   d. short-term memory

_____ 12. Processes involved in getting information into short-term memory and keeping it there are
   a. chunking and coding
   b. scanning and rehearsal
   c. categorization and interference
   d. coding and retrieval

_____ 13. The connecting link between short-term and long-term memory appears to be the part of the brain called the
   a. thalamus
   b. hypothalamus
   c. cerebellum
   d. hippocampus

_____ 14. The "tip of the tongue" phenomenon illustrates
   a. how information is transferred from sensory memory to short-term memory
   b. how words are forgotten
   c. the complexity of coding and retrieval and the intricate cross-referencing that exists in memory
   d. the importance of retrieval over original learning

_____ 15. When a person makes up a story as a strategy to learn a list of words, which process is most likely *not* involved?
   a. chunking
   b. coding
   c. imagery
   d. categorization

_____ 16. Providing subjects with category labels for words they are to learn and re-

member has been demonstrated to facilitate
a. interference
b. retention
c. rehearsal
d. retrieval

_____17. Which three terms are most closely related in their functional significance for memory?
a. sensory memory, short-term memory, retrieval
b. chunking, coding, retrieval
c. categorization, proactive inhibition, interference
d. recall, sensory memory, relearning

_____18. Which of the following is *not* a basic requirement for learning?
a. attention to the stimulus
b. some innate or previously learned behavior to which the new stimulus can become attached
c. a distinctive stimulus
d. stimulus generalization

_____19. A principal factor in developing a good memory is to
a. collect and organize a network of mediational units
b. pay attention to all stimuli
c. concentrate only on the distinctive stimuli in one's environment
d. try to extend one's short-term memory capacity

_____20. The fact that new learning builds on old learning is most closely related to the concept of
a. attachment units
b. rehearsal
c. short-term memory
d. retrieval

Key to Self-Test

1. (b);   2. (c);   3. (d);   4. (c);   5. (b);   6. (a); 7. (c);   8. (a);   9. (a);   10. (a);   11. (d);   12. (b); 13. (d);   14. (c);   15. (d);   16. (d);   17. (b);   18. (d);   19. (a);   20. (a)

exercises

I. Shown below is a list of ten nonsense syllables similar to those used by Ebbinghaus, plus a list of ten words. Find two students who will serve as subjects; have the first student study the list of nonsense syllables for 30 seconds and then write as many of them as possible on a sheet of paper within a 30-second time limit. After a few seconds' rest, permit him to study the list again for 30 seconds and then write down as many syllables as he can in the same time limit. Repeat this procedure until he can write all the syllables correctly on two consecutive trials or until he has had ten trials. Mark down how many items he correctly recalls on each memory trial. Plot his scores on the graph provided on page 37 and connect the points with a solid line.

Now engage your subject in five minutes of conversation that does not involve the nonsense-syllable learning. Talk about the weather, a sporting event, a campus issue, or this psychology course. Then retest the subject, again having him write down as many of the syllables as he can remember; plot on the graph the number of syllables he recalls correctly.

Repeat this general procedure with the second subject, but have him memorize the list of words rather than the syllables. Plot the results on the same graph but connect the points with a dashed line.

Memory Lists

TAC	WEEDS
MIH	SKY
BOK	BOWL
SIW	CARPET
PUR	TRAY
FEX	COLUMN
DOS	PLUG
WOL	ASHES
CUK	SCREEN
JAD	PAPER

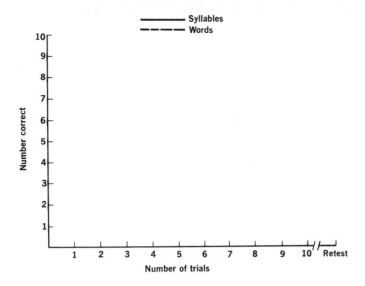

FIGURE 3–1

Questions

1. Are the curves for the syllables and words the same? If there are any differences, can you speculate why they should occur? What do the curves tell you about the learning process?
2. Which task—learning and remembering the syllables or the words—seemed easier? Can you explain why? Which list was remembered better on the retest following the five-minute break? Why?
3. Ask the two subjects about their strategy in learning these items. Did they apply any coding techniques? Which ones? Did they seem to help?
4. Would you get the same results if other subjects were tested?

II. Allow yourself five minutes to learn the nonsense syllables. Then write down as many as you can remember. When you are finished, look at the list of syllables in the test list above. Place a check next to those syllables in this list that were on the list of ten that you studied.

Test List

_____PUR	_____SIW
_____BOT	_____KUC
_____DAJ	_____TID
_____CUK	_____WUL
_____TAK	_____TAC
_____MIK	_____BOK
_____JAD	_____MIH
_____DOS	_____WOL
_____GUR	_____FEX
_____WIS	_____FAX

Questions

1. Did you get more correct with one method of memory assessment than with the other? What are these two methods called?
2. Speculate why there might be a difference in effectiveness between these two methods. If you found a difference, do you think this implies that there are two different kinds of memory or just two ways of assessing it?

CHAPTER 4

efficiency in Learning

programed unit

1. *Management of learning* is the term used to describe the attempt to arrange the most favorable possible conditions for learning to take place. When we attempt to improve efficiency in learning, we are engaged in

   _____ ____ _____.

   management of learning

2. Learning can be made more efficient by manipulating the three requirements for learning discussed in Chapter 3. You will recall that there is nothing so vital to the learning process as the storehouse of information we already possess. Such retained information serves as *attachment units* for new stimuli. Thus, being able to integrate and

   associate new information with existing _____

   attachment

   _____ is an important principle in the _____

   of learning.

   units, management

3. There are several specific ways in which this general principle works. For example, integrating a new stimulus with attachment units is easier if the stimulus is *familiar*. Rats reared in cages decorated with circles and triangles learned to discriminate between these forms more rapidly than rats reared in bare cages because the stimuli in the learning task

   were more _____ to them.

   familiar

4. A new stimulus is also more easily attached to something we already know and thus easier to learn when it is *meaningful*. A list of words is easier to learn than a list of nonsense syllables because words are

   more _____.

   meaningful

5. New material can also be learned more easily if it is learned by *rule* rather than by rote. We tend to forget rather quickly the material we learn by rote, or sheer repetition, but we tend to remember material we

learn by _____, that is, with an understanding of the meaningfulness or logical pattern that underlies it.   *rule*

6. One great aid to learning is the *guidance* that a teacher or textbook provides by relating new material to what is familiar and meaningful and by helping the student learn not by rote but by logical rule. A teacher who makes new material seem familiar, meaningful, and logical

   is providing _____.   *guidance*

7. Sometimes when we are called on to learn something that does not have much meaning, rather than learn the material by rote we make up a *mnemonic* device to help us. The jingle that begins "Thirty days hath September" is a memory crutch of this kind; it aids learning by helping us fit relatively nonlogical material into a meaningful context. This

   jingle is a _____ device.   *mnemonic*

8. *Review*
   a. The attempt to arrange the most favorable possible conditions for

      learning to take place is called _____ _____   *management of*

      _____.   *learning*

   b. Nothing is more important to learning than the storehouse of infor-

      mation we already possess, which serves as _____   *attachment*

      _____ for new stimuli.   *units*

   c. There are several specific ways in which this general principle works. For example, it is easier for English-speaking people to learn French than Russian partially because the French alphabet is more

      _____ than the Russian.   *familiar*

   d. It is easier to learn 200 words of English prose than 200 nonsense

      syllables because the prose is more _____.   *meaningful*

   e. It is easier to learn a series of numbers if we grasp some general principle in the order of the numbers than if we merely try to memorize the series mechanically, because it is more efficient to

      learn by _____ than to learn by rote.   *rule*

   f. Making new material seem familiar and meaningful and learning by

      rule rather than by rote may be facilitated by the _____   *guidance*
      of a good textbook or teacher.

   g. A memory crutch that aids rote learning by imposing a meaningful

      pattern on nonlogical material is a _____ device.   *mnemonic*

9. The second requirement for efficient learning involves paying *attention* to the stimulus. Daydreaming while studying does not promote learning

   because we are not paying _____ to the relevant   *attention*
   stimuli.

10. One way to promote attention is by increasing a person's *motivation* to learn. If the subject matter is related to a person's motives, he is likely to pay more attention to it. If you know you are going to Mexico next summer, you might study your Spanish more intensely because you

    have greater _____ to learn it.   motivation

11. Another aid to paying attention is *feedback*. Feedback constitutes information on how well the learning process is going. In this Guide, revealing the correct answer after writing yours in the blank provides

    immediate _____ on the progress of your learning.   feedback

12. Feedback promotes learning for two major reasons. First, it enables the learner to correct any mistakes quickly. Second, when the learner can see that progress is being made he becomes more interested in the task and his motivation for learning increases. Therefore,

    _____ helps capture and hold attention.   feedback

13. *Reward* also captures and directs attention and is effective in the management of learning. A parent who smiles and pats an infant who

    has just uttered his first word is providing a _____ for this   reward
    behavior.

14. There are two general kinds of reward. One group is called *external rewards*. These rewards originate outside the organism. Food, a college

    diploma, money, and parental praise are examples of _____   external

    _____.   rewards

15. In contrast, the second group is called *internal rewards*. These rewards originate within the organism. Feelings of satisfaction, power, and

    charity are _____ _____.   internal rewards

16. If you study psychology because you want a good grade, your attention

    to it is reinforced by an _____ _____. Con-   external reward
    versely, if you learn because you are interested in the material for

    its own sake, your attention is maintained by _____   internal

    _____.   rewards

17. Another tool used in the management of learning is *punishment*. A slap on the hand or the disapproval of one's friends constitutes

    _____.   punishment

18. Punishment as well as reward may call attention to relevant stimuli in a learning situation. If a young child is about to wander into the street,

a sharp "No!" from his parent constitutes a _____   punishment
and focuses attention on the dangerous act.

19. *Novelty* is another means of attracting and focusing attention. For a
child from northern Michigan a palm tree may be fascinating, but for a
Florida youth snow, not palm trees, attracts rapt interest. Thus we are
likely to pay attention to something and learn about it if that event has

_____.   novelty

20. *Review*
   a. An important requirement for learning is that the stimuli for learning

   attract the _____ of the learner. Attention may   attention
   be recruited and focused if the subject matter relates to the in-

   dividual's needs and _____.   motivation
   b. Another aid to capturing and holding attention is information on the

   progress of learning, or _____.   feedback
   c. Attention is focused on the learning situation if correct responses

   are followed by a _____. Praise from a teacher is an   reward

   _____ reward, while a feeling of satisfaction in having   external

   performed well is an _____ reward.   internal

   d. Not only reward for correct responses but _____ of   punishment
   incorrect responses can direct attention.

   e. If a stimulus stands out because of its uniqueness or _____,   novelty
   it is likely to be attended to and learned more easily than other stimuli
   in that context.

21. One more requirement for learning, the need for a *distinctive* stimulus,
also relates to the management of learning. We need to consider ways
in which the learning stimulus can be made to stand out, or can be made

more _____, and therefore easier to learn.   distinctive

22. A characteristic of the learning stimulus that has an important effect
on the learning process is *serial position*. Serial position refers to the
order of an item in a series, that is, whether it occurs at the beginning,
middle, or end. In any series of stimuli, we tend to learn the first and
last items best. Therefore, which items are most distinctive and easiest

to learn and remember is partly determined by their _____   serial

_____.   position

23. The law of *primacy* refers to the tendency for items at the beginning of a learning task (those that have primacy) to be more easily
remembered. The fact that in a series of nonsense syllables the first

few are likely to be remembered more easily describes the law of

_____.   primacy

24. *Recency* also determines which items are learned best. Items that we learn last (that have recency) tend to be remembered more easily according to the law of _____.   recency

25. Suppose you are to learn the following list of seven syllables: KIB, YOB, MOX, KEP, RUS, CIZ, PAV. It is likely that all the items will not be remembered equally well because of the effects of _____   serial

_____. You might remember KIB and YOB more easily   position

than MOX and KEP, as the law of _____ suggests, and   primacy

remember CIZ and PAV more easily according to the law of _____.   recency

26. The strategy a person adopts in attempting to learn new material also affects the efficiency of learning. One approach to learning is called the *whole* method. Learning by this procedure involves studying the material in its entirety rather than breaking it up into smaller parts. Reading an entire chapter in a textbook over and over again illustrates

studying by the _____ method.   whole

27. An alternative approach is the *part* method. This procedure is characterized by breaking up the material to be learned into smaller parts that are studied separately. Very long material often may profitably be

broken into sections and studied by the _____ method.   part

28. The whole method is advantageous when the material is relatively brief and has some logical structure to it. The part method is more appropriate for learning long material. A textbook chapter is generally both logically organized and long; so perhaps the most efficient approach to

studying it might be a combination of the _____ and _____   whole, part
methods.

29. One combination of the whole and part methods is the *progressive part* method, which is especially helpful in learning passages word for word. The material is broken into parts. The first part is learned, then the second. Then the first and second parts are rehearsed together in sequence. Next the third part is added, and so on. A good strategy for

learning a speech or memorizing a poem would be the _____   progressive

_____ method.   part

30. Additional trials on which we continue to study something that we have already learned contribute to *overlearning,* which often aids retention. For instance, in childhood we listen over and over again to favorite

fairy tales; frequently adults can remember the precise words of the fairy tales they learned years earlier because of _____.

overlearning

31. One method of study is *massed practice,* or a single, unbroken period of study. Cramming for an exam is an example of _____ _____.

massed

practice

32. In contrast, *distributed practice* is a series of shorter learning sessions, with rest periods in between. The notion of studying a little psychology each day illustrates the principle of _____ _____.

distributed

practice

33. Distributed practice is usually preferable to massed practice because fatigue and boredom are reduced and covert rehearsal frequently occurs during the rest periods. Generally, the most efficient strategy is to break up your study time, or use _____ _____ rather than _____ _____.

distributed

practice, massed practice

34. *Recitation* is simply either silent or oral rehearsal. Reading followed by an active attempt to restate the major ideas in your own words, called _____, is a very efficient study method.

recitation

35. It has been found that devoting as much as 80 percent of study time to silent or oral rehearsal of the material, or to _____, is a far more efficient method of learning than merely reading the material over and over.

recitation

36. *Review*
   a. In addition to the possession of attachment units and the need for paying attention to the relevant stimuli, a third requirement for learning is a _____ stimulus.

distinctive

   b. Not all words in a list are learned equally well; how well they are learned depends on their _____ _____ in the list. The first words are more distinctive and learned more easily according to the law of _____, while the last words are learned more easily according to the law of _____.

serial position

primacy

recency

   c. Large blocks of material can be made more distinctive by using a specific learning strategy. For example, if the material to be learned is relatively short and has a logical structure, the preferred learning strategy might be to study it in its entirety, by the _____ method. Conversely, if the material is quite long, the better approach might be to break it up into smaller units, or learn by the

whole

_____ method. A combination of these procedures that is
helpful in memorizing material word for word is the _____
_____ method.

    d. Additional study after one has already learned something increases
retention because of _____ .

    e. Spacing one's practice sessions, called _____
_____ , is generally more efficient than a single
long learning session, or _____ _____ .

    f. Reading followed by oral or silent rehearsal of the material, or
_____ , is a very efficient study method.

part

progressive
part

overlearning

distributed

practice

massed practice

recitation

37. The influence that learning one task has on the learning of another is
called *transfer*. Formerly, people thought that learning Latin or Greek
assisted the learning of other subjects, but this theory has been dis-
proved. However, new learning is sometimes made easier or more
difficult because of the influence of other learning; in other words,

    _____ does take place.　　　　　　　　　　transfer

38. When the learning of a second task (task 2) is facilitated by having
learned a previous task (task 1), the effect is called *positive transfer*.
A young child who learns to ride a tricycle will find later that learning

    to ride a bicycle is easier because of _____ _____ .　positive transfer

39. On the other hand, when task 2 is harder to learn because of having
previously learned task 1, the effect is known as *negative transfer*. Knowing how to steer a car frequently makes learning to operate the tiller

    of a boat more difficult because of _____ _____ .　negative transfer

40. When we learn, we also develop *learning sets;* that is, we "learn to
learn," or develop attitudes and strategies that help us in similar learning situations in the future. If you become proficient at a certain type
of task, even though particular aspects of that task may change, you

    have developed a _____ _____ for that task.　　learning set

41. In an experimental illustration of the development of a learning set,
a monkey was supposed to discriminate between two objects, one of
which had food beneath it. At first the monkey took quite a few trials
to learn, but after many examples of this type of problem, it finally
became able to solve each new problem in a single trial. The monkey

    had developed a _____ _____ for solving this kind　learning set
of problem.

42. *Review*
    a. The influence that learning one task has on the learning of another

is called _____. If learning task 2 is facilitated by   transfer

first learning task 1, _____ _____   positive transfer
has occurred. If learning task 1 hinders the subsequent learning

of task 2, _____ _____ has occurred.   negative transfer

   b. "Learning to learn" describes the development of a _____   learning

_____.   set

43. One approach to improving efficiency in the classroom has been the
development of *programed* instruction, in which the contents of a
course are broken down into very small steps. This Study Guide is an

   example of _____ instruction.   programed

44. Programed material may be in printed form, as in this Guide, or it may
be presented to a student by a *teaching machine.* A simple, manually

   operated device or an electronic computer may serve as a _____   teaching

_____.   machine

45. A teaching machine presents one *frame,* or step, at a time. At his own

   rate the student completes each _____ before going on to   frame
the next.

46. The use of programed instruction and teaching machines has apparent
advantages, especially for the below-average student. The student can

   proceed at his own pace, since he controls when the next _____   frame
is presented, he is individually instructed, and he receives immediate
feedback on the progress of learning.

self-test

_____ 1. The term *management of learning* applies to the attempt to
   a. control what students learn
   b. arrange the conditions that create
greatest efficiency in learning
   c. determine the reinforcements that
will increase appropriate and de-
crease inappropriate learning
   d. structure the classroom so that
students will learn a few things
very well

_____ 2. Familiarity with the stimulus and

meaningfulness of the material assist
in learning mainly by providing
   a. guidance
   b. mnemonic devices
   c. attachment units
   d. novelty

_____ 3. Relative to nonsense syllables of "low
association value," syllables of "high
association value" can be learned
   a. more easily because they represent
novel stimuli
   b. more easily because they can be

readily attached to existing mediational units

c. less easily because one syllable
tends to be confused with another

d. less easily because we have to
remember the mnemonic devices
we create

_____ 4. Learning by rote is
a. referred to as "chunking"
b. always discouraged by a good
teacher
c. less efficient than learning by rule
d. slower than learning by rule but
leads to remembering the material
longer

_____ 5. The major role of guidance in learning
is to
a. point out what is familiar, meaningful, and best learned by logical
rule
b. select a few basic principles to be
learned
c. show the quickest method for
learning certain materials
d. determine the most appropriate
reinforcements

_____ 6. Certain evidence suggests that the
amount learned depends on the
a. total time spent studying
b. proportional time spent studying
the material in relation to other
materials being studied during
the same period
c. spacing of the practice sessions
d. all of the above

_____ 7. In many learning situations, reinforcement and feedback are similar in that
they both
a. motivate the learner
b. provide information on the correct-
ness of a response
c. focus attention on relevant stimuli
d. all of the above

_____ 8. An example of an internal reward is
a. food
b. praise

c. satisfaction of curiosity
d. a mother's smile

_____ 9. Novelty that is appropriately used
is important in learning because of
its ability to
a. summon attachment units
b. reduce the delay of reinforcement
c. provide feedback
d. focus attention on the relevant
stimulus

_____ 10. The laws of primacy and recency
suggest that learning might be more
efficient if
a. there is very little delay of reward
b. feedback is immediate and distinctive
c. the material is broken up into
smaller units
d. practice is distributed rather than
massed

_____ 11. An effective method for learning
the logic and detail of long textual
material like a chapter in a history
textbook is the
a. whole method
b. part method
c. rote method
d. whole method followed by the
part method

_____ 12. The law of overlearning says that
a. most learning that occurs in every-
day life is seldom forgotten
b. cramming leads to adequate learning if the material is logical and
meaningful
c. massed practice results in better
retention
d. additional practice after material
can barely be recalled produces
greater retention

_____ 13. The fact that fatigue inhibits the
progress of learning helps explain the
effects of
a. overlearning and feedback
b. distributed practice and the part
method

c. internal reward and massed practice

d. primacy and the progressive part method

_____14. In distributed practice, the learner may covertly rehearse the material during the rest periods, which leads to
a. consolidation
b. differential forgetting
c. positive transfer
d. learning sets

_____15. Differential forgetting may be one beneficial result of
a. short delays in reinforcement
b. distributed practice
c. massed practice
d. recitation

_____16. Distributed practice
a. is less helpful when learning by rule than when learning by rote
b. is most helpful when a great deal of "cranking up" is required (for example, assembling study materials and reviewing notes)
c. promotes retention better than massed practice
d. interferes with differential forgetting

_____17. Attitudes and strategies that help us perform in particular types of learning situations are called
a. learning sets
b. overlearning
c. mediated transfer
d. retroactive inhibition

_____18. A parental attitude of "spare the rod and spoil the child" may produce

a. socially disciplined children
b. "learned helplessness"
c. passive children
d. achieving but aggressive children

_____19. The Coleman Report indicated that a major factor in the failure of children from low-income families to succeed in school is the
a. pupils' poor self-concept and lack of a feeling of control over their environments
b. poor salaries paid teachers
c. lack of modern teaching methods in the schools
d. lack of modern buildings and laboratory facilities

_____20. A study that compared the effects of reward and punishment on the learning performance of lower- and middle-class boys showed that the performance of lower-class boys was helped by
a. both reward for correct answers and punishment for incorrect responses
b. reward but not influenced by punishment
c. punishment but not influenced by reward
d. reward but hindered by punishment

Key to Self-Test

1. (b); 2. (c); 3. (b); 4. (c); 5. (a); 6. (d); 7. (d); 8. (c); 9. (d); 10. (c); 11. (d); 12. (d); 13. (b); 14. (a); 15. (b); 16. (a); 17. (a); 18. (b); 19. (a); 20. (d)

exercises

I. Although much of the discussion of learning has involved laboratory demonstrations and experiments, the principles of learning function just as effectively in common social situations. Some psychologists view childhood as a period during which the child acquires social skills through the ordinary principles of learning—reward, punishment, observation, extinction, generalization, and so on. For example, parents frequently use praise, smiles, money, and candy to reward behavior that they want repeated more often. They also use words of displeasure, spanking, and threatening glances as punishments for inappropriate behavior. Sometimes a parent will ignore a certain response in order to extinguish it.

Below are three situations in which appropriate social behavior could be taught to a child by employing the principles of learning that you have been studying. Although there is no agreement among psychologists on the best procedure, describe and explain some of the ways in which you as a parent might try to guide your child in these situations.

1. Your child throws a temper tantrum every time he does not get his own way.
2. It is time to toilet train your child. How would you go about it?
3. Your child is continually playing with his food, spreading it all over the table and sometimes throwing it. Since he is old enough to control his eating behavior, how would you train him?

II. On page 37 of this Guide is a test list of twenty nonsense syllables. Pick one friend and give him *six* minutes to learn the list. Test for learning by allowing the subject two minutes to write down as many syllables as possible. Engage the subject in conversation that is irrelevant to the learning task and pretend that the experiment is over. Then, after five minutes, ask the subject to write as many syllables as possible in two minutes.

Next pick a second subject and provide an initial learning period of *two* minutes. Then have the subject copy a picture or design (for example, a cartoon character or a complex geometric pattern), giving him a time limit of two minutes (do not make the drawing task so easy that it can be finished in this length of time). Permit the subject two more minutes to learn the same list of syllables, again followed by a different drawing task for two minutes. Finally, allow two additional minutes of study followed by the same test as for the first subject. Engage the individual in irrelevant conversation for five minutes and retest.

Questions

1. Which subject did better on the first test? Why?
2. Which subject did better on the retest? Why?
3. Explain the possible roles of massed versus distributed practice, fatigue, covert rehearsal, and interference.

III. The exercises for Chapter 3 suggested performing an experiment in which subjects were to memorize lists of nonsense syllables and words. One task was to note the difference in the ability to learn and remember the syllables as opposed to the words. Presumably this difference was a function of a greater network of mediational units for the words as opposed to the syllables. One way to assess the nature of the mediational units that aid in learning verbal material is to examine the *mnemonic devices* that people use in the learning process. As you will recall, a mnemonic device is usually a set of associations between items to be learned. If a person is trying to remember the words *house, sky,* and *blanket,* he may create the mnemonic device "I sleep covered with my *blanket* in my *house* under a clear *sky*."

Ask a friend to learn the lists on page 36 of this Guide. Allow him six minutes to study the list of words and one minute to recall them. After he has finished writing as many items as he can recall, ask him how he went about learning them. Did he use any "gimmicks" to assist him or did he just learn them by rote? Be sure to ask how he tried to learn items that he did not recall correctly as well as those he did remember. Then have him learn the list of nonsense syllables in the same manner. Again ask about the use of mnemonics.

In general, did he remember the items for which he had mnemonic devices better than those for which he did not have a special memory gimmick? Do you feel that some of his mnemonic devices hindered rather than helped his learning and memory? What is the nature of a good mnemonic device?

CHAPTER 5

Language, thinking, and problem solving

programed unit

1. *Language* is a special form of behavior that enables man to communicate an almost infinite variety of messages. Although other animals can communicate with one another, man alone uses highly complex and symbolic _____.

   language

2. Man is distinguished from other animals by the fact that he can convey through language an almost endless number of unique thoughts. Therefore man can pass enormous amounts of knowledge from one generation to the next by using _____.

   language

3. The building blocks of speech, or spoken language, are *phonemes*. Phonemes are basic sounds. For example, "ah" and "th" are basic sounds and are among the _____ of English.

   phonemes

4. All languages are built on phonemes. English has forty-five, the simplest language known has fifteen, and no language has more than eighty-five _____.

   phonemes

5. Phonemes have no meaning by themselves—they are just elementary sounds. However, *morphemes* are basic combinations of these sounds that possess meaning. A meaningful combination of phonemes constitutes a _____.

   morpheme

6. Morphemes may be words. While the sounds "t," "ee," and "ch" are all _____, "teach," a meaningful combination of these sounds, is a _____ that is a word.

   phonemes

   morpheme

7. Morphemes may also be prefixes and suffixes and may be combined with other morphemes to form new words. The prefix "un-" and the

suffix "-able," which are _____ because they possess meaning, can be combined with the morpheme "teach" to form the new word "unteachable."   *morphemes*

8. The most important feature of language is the manner in which phonemes and morphemes are combined into meaningful utterances through *grammar*. Rules that dictate the meaningful combinations of

   sounds and words in a language constitute its _____.   *grammar*

9. A child's early attempts at language communication are *telegraphic;* that is, the child uses only words most important to his meaning and often omits the articles, adjectives, and verbs. A young child pointing

   to a bird in a tree might say, "Bird . . . tree," an example of _____ speech.   *telegraphic*

10. Another characteristic of a child's speech is that it is *holophrastic.* That is, the child uses a single word to represent an entire idea or sentence. A two-year-old pointing to the cookie jar and imploringly shouting,

    "cookie" to mean "please give me a cookie," is using _____ speech.   *holophrastic*

11. *Review*
    a. The basic sounds of language, called _____,   *phonemes*

    are combined into meaningful units known as _____,   *morphemes*
    which alone or in combination are the words of a language.
    b. The meaningful combination of phonemes and morphemes to form

    sentences is dictated by the rules of _____.   *grammar*
    c. Children often omit words not important to their meaning; that

    is, they use _____ speech. They may also   *telegraphic*
    say a single word to stand for an entire sentence, which is known as

    _____ speech.   *holophrastic*

12. Although many nouns stand for particular objects, others denote a whole class of objects, events, or ideas and are called *concepts.* A concept is a symbol for a common characteristic or relationship shared by objects or events that are otherwise different. "Medicine," "justice," and "book"

    are all _____.   *concepts*

13. Children apparently first learn concepts of definite objects and of shapes and only later learn more abstract concepts. Therefore, there appears

    to be a sequence in which children acquire _____.   *concepts*

14. For adults, concepts tend to be cross-classified; that is, the concepts suggest various objects, events, or ideas. However, the first and presumably most important definition a concept brings to mind is based

on what is called its *salient characteristic,* or its outstanding feature. To a theologian the word "man" might suggest "a child of God," whereas to a physician it might imply a "functioning collection of physiological apparatus." The word "man" does not have the same _____ _____ for the theologian and the physician.

salient
characteristic

15. For one person a tree may call forth the concept of "a thing of beauty," but to another it is "the largest plant." Again, there is a difference in the _____ _____ of the word "tree."

salient characteristic

16. The associations that make up concepts are arranged in a *concept hierarchy.* When one thinks of the concept "animal" the first association that comes to mind might be "dog," followed by "cat," "horse," and, much later, "llama." This ordering of associations is known as a _____ _____.

concept
hierarchy

17. The implication of such a hierarchy is that the first association one thinks of is more strongly related to the concept in one's mind than each subsequent association. Therefore, a list of the associations to a concept in their order of strength defines a _____ _____.

concept
hierarchy

18. Most words and concepts have additional implied meanings called *connotations.* The word "mother-in-law" simply means the mother of one's spouse, but clearly people also have evaluative feelings that accompany the concept (for example, unpleasant, interfering, strong-minded). These implied meanings are _____.

connotations

19. An instrument used to measure the implied meanings, or connotations, of words and concepts is the *semantic differential.* Most people can describe their feelings about a concept by rating it as more or less good or bad, strong or weak, and so on. An instrument that attempts to measure these _____ is the _____ _____.

connotations, semantic
differential

20. *Review*
    a. Some nouns denote a whole class of objects, events, or ideas and are called _____.

concepts

    b. Adults may regard a word as belonging to several conceptual classifications. However, each person has his own primary definition of a concept based on what is to him its most outstanding feature, or _____ _____.

salient characteristic

c. The associations a concept brings to mind, listed in order of their strength, constitute a _____ _____.   concept hierarchy

d. In addition to their objective meanings, concepts have implied meanings known as _____.   connotations

e. The different connotative meanings a concept has can be measured by the _____ _____.   semantic differential

21. *Thinking* is the mental manipulation of images, symbols, concepts, rules, and other mediational units. When someone says "apple" you might call forth a mental image of an apple. This simple manipulation of an image is an elementary illustration of _____.   thinking

22. Recall that a *mediational unit* is an association within the brain. One of the mediational units manipulated in thinking is the *image,* or the recollection of a sensory experience. It is remarkable that Beethoven wrote much of his most famous music after he was deaf. Apparently he possessed the ability to mentally create and manipulate tonal

_____.   images

23. In addition, much of thinking is the manipulation of symbols, particularly *words* and *concepts.* Man is capable of labeling the objects and events in his environment and thus mentally manipulating them without

seeing or touching them; he does this through the use of _____.   words
He is able to treat them as groups with a common characteristic through

the use of _____.   concepts

24. Images, words, and concepts are all _____   mediational

_____that can be manipulated in the course of _____.   units, thinking

25. *Review*
a. The mental manipulation of mediational units is called _____.   thinking

b. These mediational units are often _____, _____,   images, words

and _____.   concepts

26. There are at least two general kinds of thinking process. The first is thinking by means of *logical rules.* Formal reasoning and simple deductions and inferences would be thinking according to _____   logical

_____.   rules

27. One formal logical thought process is called a *syllogism.* It often follows the form: "All A is B, C is A, therefore C is B." For example, the argument "All men are mortal, I am a man, therefore I am mortal" is a

_____.   syllogism

28. A syllogism usually begins with two *premises*. A premise is a statement of belief or fact. "All men are mortal" and "I am a man" are statements of belief that also happen to be true facts. They are the _____ premises

of the _____ in frame 27.   syllogism

29. The final statement in a syllogism is its *conclusion*. It must follow unequivocally from the premises. In the above argument, "I am mortal" is

the _____.   conclusion

30. Although the conclusion must follow from the premises, it is not necessarily a true fact. The conclusion may be false if one or both premises are false. For example, "All girls are romantic, Jane is a girl, therefore Jane is romantic" constitutes a logical argument, but because of a false

_____ its _____ may not be true.   premise, conclusion

31. Therefore, a general rule is that the _____ of   conclusion

a formal syllogism is true only if both _____ are also   premises
true.

32. In contrast to the formal logic of a syllogism, another method of thinking is a more personal and less precise form of association described by the term *mediational cluster*. We have said that most words are cross-indexed under many different concepts, and in turn one concept may be more or less associated with other concepts, and so on. The entire network of associated words, concepts, and connotations forms a

_____ _____.   mediational cluster

33. Mediational clusters operate in the following way: Suppose a person were asked to think of the word "angel." First, he might think of a girl in flowing robes with wings, then about a harp, which might then lead to thoughts of music and perhaps of an orchestra playing religious music, and so on. This grouping of mediational units is known as a

_____ _____.   mediational cluster

34. In addition to the methods of thinking represented by logic and by mediational clusters, thinking may be divided into two general types. The first kind is *undirected thinking*. Undirected thinking occurs somewhat spontaneously and does not converge on a particular goal, such as a "right answer." Thinking that appears to take place spontaneously

and without a specific goal is called _____ thinking.   undirected

35. When we daydream, our thoughts seem to occur spontaneously. We make associations between images and symbols that have no logical

relationship. Daydreaming is an example of _____   undirected
thinking.

36. Conversely, *directed thinking* is something we deliberately do with a specific goal in mind. Coming up with the correct answer to a question in the Self-Test involves _____ thinking.

    directed

37. The type of thinking that is most closely related to mediational clusters and the workings of the imagination is _____ thinking. A satisfactory performance on an achievement test usually requires _____ thinking.

    undirected

    directed

38. *Review*
    a. A precise and disciplined method of thinking involves systematic relationships or _____ _____.

        logical rules

    b. One example of logical thinking is the formal _____, which is typically composed of two _____ and a _____.

        syllogism

        premises

        conclusion

    c. A second method of thinking involves the more personal and less precise network of associations among mediational units known as a _____ _____.

        mediational cluster

    d. A spontaneous type of thinking not focused on a specific "right answer" is called _____ thinking, while goal-oriented thinking is termed _____ thinking.

        undirected

        directed

39. Much directed thinking takes the form of *problem solving*. Determining the fastest route to drive between two distant cities is an example of _____ _____.

    problem solving

40. When confronted with a simple problem, lower animals usually demonstrate *trial and error* behavior. First they try one solution, it fails, they shift to another, it fails, and so on, until they solve the problem. The overt attempt at one solution and then another is called _____ _____ _____.

    trial

    and error

41. Higher animals, particularly man, are more likely to solve a problem by *insight* than by trial and error. This behavior appears to be a sudden exhibition of the correct response with little if any overt trial and error. An example is the chimpanzee that suddenly piled boxes on top of one another to reach a bunch of bananas hanging high above its head. It solved the problem by _____.

    insight

42. The major difference between trial and error and insight is not only that insight seems to lead to a faster solution but also that in the thinking process preceding the insightful behavior a great deal of covert

rather than overt trial and error goes on. If the solution to a problem is arrived at by overtly trying one potential solution and then another,

this is called _____ _____ _____; but if whatever   trial and error
trial and error there may be is carried out covertly by the manipulation

of symbols it is called _____.   insight

43. A factor that often affects problem solving is *persistence of set*. In developing learning sets (discussed in Chapter 4), we learn to solve problems of a given type in a certain manner. When we confront a new example of that general type of problem we attack it in a similar fashion.

This tendency is called _____ ____ _____.   persistence of set

44. Persistence of set becomes a barrier to problem solving when the new problem looks similar to the old one but actually requires a new procedure. The result is that the old procedure may be applied again and again and new and more efficient methods overlooked entirely. Therefore, although it may be beneficial in solving old problems,

_____ ____ _____ frequently interferes with   persistence of set
discovering a creative solution to a new task.

45. A special type of persistence of set is *functional fixedness*, which also reduces our efficiency at problem solving. This is the tendency to think of objects as functioning in only one way and not others. People who cannot think of creative uses for a hammer, such as a doorstop,

crowbar, ice crusher, and so on, may be demonstrating a _____   functional

_____ in their thinking about the hammer.   fixedness

46. *Review*
a. One major example of directed thinking is _____   problem

_____.   solving
b. There are two general approaches to problem solving. If the solution is discovered after much overt exploration and manipulation, the

method is called _____ _____ _____. Conversely,   trial and error
if the problem is suddenly solved with a minimum of overt trial and

error, the method is called _____.   insight
c. One barrier to solving new problems is to continue to apply old methods of solving similar problems. This is a tendency known as

_____ ____ _____.   persistence of set

d. A special form of set is the tendency to think of objects as functioning in only one way, called _____   functional

_____.   fixedness

self-test

_____ 1. The difference between man's communication system and that of lower animals is that man
   a. communicates meaning
   b. can communicate by using symbols
   c. uses vocal sounds
   d. has a language that permits the expression of an almost infinite variety of thoughts

_____ 2. Once a child has learned the meaning of the word "toy," he readily associates objects as physically different as a rubber ball and a bicycle. This process is called
   a. syntactic analysis
   b. discrimination of salient characteristics
   c. mediated generalization
   d. persistence of set

_____ 3. A phoneme is
   a. a word
   b. a syllable
   c. a basic sound
   d. the smallest meaningful unit of language

_____ 4. A morpheme may be a
   a. word
   b. combination of phonemes
   c. suffix
   d. all of the above

_____ 5. The development of babbling in the first two months of life seems to
   a. depend on the verbal stimulation of the parents
   b. depend on the reinforcement of English-like sounds emitted by the child
   c. occur spontaneously
   d. none of the above

_____ 6. A major problem for theorists who attempt to explain language development by simple conditioning or observation learning is the fact that
   a. children from different nations learn different languages
   b. children apply grammatical rules at such an early age
   c. children acquire a vocabulary so quickly
   d. infants produce so many phonemes

_____ 7. A symbol that stands for a common characteristic or relationship shared by several objects or events is a
   a. phoneme
   b. participle
   c. concept
   d. morpheme

_____ 8. Suppose someone thinks of the notion of strength when shown the word "athlete." This implied meaning is a
   a. connotation
   b. concept hierarchy
   c. holophrastic generalization
   d. persistence of set

_____ 9. A tool for measuring the connotative meanings of a concept is called
   a. a didactic instrument
   b. the semantic differential
   c. the Osgood Test of Salient Characteristics
   d. none of the above

_____ 10. The mental manipulation of mediational units best describes
   a. thinking
   b. concept hierarchies
   c. the search for salient characteristics
   d. trial and error learning

_____ 11. The essential difference between a fact and a premise is based on whether or not
   a. most people have substantial faith in its validity
   b. one's logical thinking embraces it
   c. one's overt behavior depends on it
   d. it is useful

_____12. In a syllogism
    a. the conclusion is always true
    b. the conclusion is true if the premises are true
    c. the premises are always true
    d. it is impossible to have a false premise but a true conclusion

_____13. If you commented on the heat of the evening and your friend responded with, "That reminds me of . . .," followed by a long discourse beginning with his trip to Africa and ending with his athletic prowess, your friend illustrated the concept of
    a. salient characteristics
    b. directed thinking
    c. syllogistic thinking
    d. mediational clustering

_____14. The difference between trial and error and insight is centered on the
    a. fact that no errors in thinking have been made if the problem is solved by insight
    b. accuracy of the result
    c. number of overt attempts made at solving the problem
    d. fact that only man demonstrates insight in solving problems

_____15. In problem solving, a hypothesis is usually a(n)
    a. educated guess about the solution
    b. tried and tested solution
    c. solution that must follow on the basis of syllogistic reasoning
    d. wild speculation

_____16. Persistence of set is best characterized as a
    a. barrier to solving familiar problems
    b. help in undirected thinking
    c. hindrance to solving all problems
    d. hindrance to solving new types but not old types of problems

_____17. Functional fixedness is a
    a. motor impairment
    b. special form of set
    c. type of mediational clustering
    d. mediated generalization

_____18. Creative people tend to be
    a. popular
    b. generally unconcerned with what others think of them
    c. passive
    d. concerned with success

_____19. A creative product is best characterized as being
    a. bizarre
    b. unique
    c. strange
    d. novel but appropriate

_____20. Of the following, which two concepts are most similar and functionally related to each other?
    a. mediational clustering and undirected thinking
    b. persistence of set and creativity
    c. problem solving and connotations
    d. concept hierarchies and functional fixedness

Key to Self-Test

1. (d); 2. (c); 3. (c); 4. (d); 5. (c); 6. (b); 7. (c); 8. (a); 9. (b); 10. (a); 11. (a); 12. (b); 13. (d); 14. (c); 15. (a); 16. (d); 17. (b); 18. (b); 19. (d); 20. (a)

exercise

On pages 58–59 are eight forms of the semantic differential scales devised by C. E. Osgood to measure the connotations (or implied meanings) that words and concepts have of such qualities as goodness or badness, strength or weakness, activity or passivity, and so on. Use these forms to get ratings from several of your friends on some or all of the following concepts:

psychology   war
government   social action
advertising   clothing
adopting children   dedication in life

Write the concept to be rated in the space provided above each form.

Have your subjects place a dot along each line, as between "good" and "bad," at a point that describes their relative feelings about the concept you give them. By drawing a line from point to point, you may then construct a profile of what the concept connotes to each subject. Next you may get ratings of the same word from several subjects or pool your findings with other members of your class in order to make up a group profile for the concept. Use as scores the numbers 1 through 7 along the bottom of the form. The group score on each line will be at the point corresponding to the average of the numbers for the dots placed on the line by your subjects. You will probably find it interesting to get one group

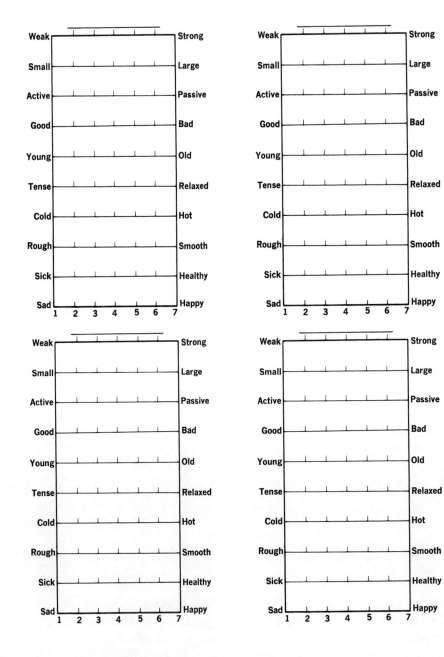

score for male subjects and another for female subjects for each of the eight concepts.

Questions

1. Examine the ratings for each concept. How are they different? Discuss and explain the nature of these differences. Do these ratings reflect what you feel to be true about these concepts?

2. Did people show less agreement in rating some concepts than others? Why?

3. Look separately at the profiles made by each sex. On which concepts do men respond differently from women?

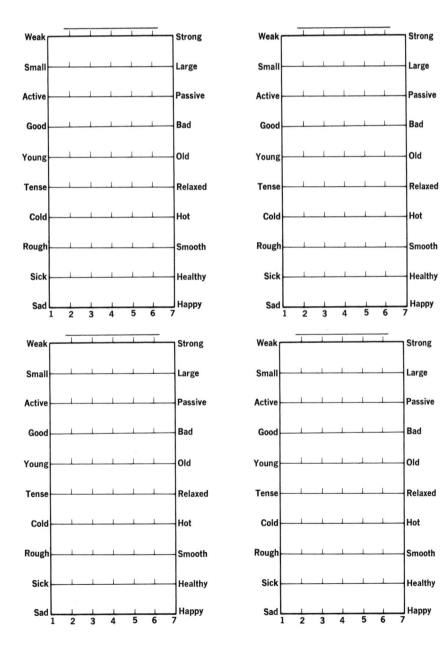

CHAPTER 6 THE SENSES

programed unit

1. There are two essential elements in the operation of the senses. The first is the occurrence of a *stimulus*. A stimulus is any form of energy capable of exciting the nervous system. The light waves reflected off

   this page constitute a _____.   stimulus

2. In addition, the stimulus must be detected by a *receptor*. Receptors are specialized nerve endings capable of responding to energy. The light-

   sensitive nerve endings in your eye are _____ for the   receptors
   stimulus of the light waves reflected off this page.

3. To cause a receptor to respond, a stimulus must have an intensity above the receptor's *absolute threshold*. The absolute threshold is the intensity at which a stimulus can be detected on 50 percent of its occurrences. If you were presented with a very faint tone that you could detect half the time, the intensity of that tone would represent your

   _____ _____ for hearing.   absolute threshold

4. A stimulus that is above the absolute threshold is termed *supraliminal*. Literally, supraliminal means "over the limen," and "limen" is another name for threshold. Since you can detect the light in the room, it is a

   _____ stimulus because it is above your   supraliminal

   _____ _____.   absolute threshold

5. In contrast, a source of energy that is detected less than 50 percent of the time is *subliminal*. Literally, it is "under the limen" or below the threshold. A tone too faint to hear, even half the time, is

   _____.   subliminal

6. Measurements establishing the precise absolute thresholds for the various senses under various conditions have been made with proce-

dures known as *psychophysical methods*. Presenting a series of tones, each one slightly louder than the preceding one, until a subject consistently reports that he hears the tone is an example of one of the

_____ _____.   psychophysical methods

7. *Review*

   a. A form of energy capable of exciting the nervous system is a

   _____. The specialized nerve endings that respond   stimulus

   to its presence are _____.   receptors

   b. The intensity at which a stimulus can be detected 50 percent of the

   time defines the _____ _____.   absolute threshold

   c. A stimulus above the absolute threshold is called _____;   supraliminal

   a stimulus below the threshold is _____.   subliminal

   d. Procedures used for precisely determining thresholds are called

   _____ _____.   psychophysical methods

8. The *difference threshold* for a receptor is the minimum difference in intensity at which a receptor can recognize a difference between two stimuli 50 percent of the time. When the average person looks at two lights, one of which is 1.6 percent brighter than the other, he can detect a difference half the time. Thus 1.6 percent is the

   _____ _____ for light.   difference threshold

9. A difference between two sounds can be detected half the time if their

   loudness varies by 10 percent. Thus 10 percent is the _____   difference

   _____ for sounds.   threshold

10. A difference threshold is reached when you detect a *just noticeable difference,* or *j.n.d.* When the intensities of two lights vary by 1.6 percent or of two sounds by 10 percent, you would detect a

    _____ _____ _____, or   just noticeable difference

    ___ ___ ___.   j.n.d.

11. The fact that the difference threshold tends to be a fixed percentage of change in intensity is called *Weber's Law.* Thus the fact that one light must be 1.6 percent brighter than another for the eye to detect a just

    noticeable difference illustrates _____ _____.   Weber's Law

12. After continued stimulation, the sensory receptors adjust to a stimulus through the process called *sensory adaptation.* That is, they "get used to" the stimulus and stop responding. You do not usually "feel" the pressure

of the watch on your wrist because of the process of _____   sensory

_____.   adaptation

13. *Review*
    a. If a light must have an intensity of 101.6 units in order for it to be
       recognized as different from a 100-unit light, the difference in in-

       tensity of 1.6 percent represents the _____   difference

       _____. You would detect a _____   threshold, just

       _____ _____.   noticeable difference

    b. If a 10-unit light is used, the greater intensity necessary to produce

       a j.n.d. would be approximately _____ units according to   10.16

       _____ _____.   Weber's Law

    c. With continued stimulation, receptors cease to respond to stimuli

       because of _____ _____.   sensory adaptation

14. The receptors responsible for the sense of taste are the *taste buds,* con-
    tained in the little bumps on the tongue and in the back of the mouth
    and in the throat. Food in solution comes in contact with nerve endings

    in the _____ _____, which then become chemically acti-   taste buds
    vated and send nervous impulses to the brain.

15. The taste receptors respond to four basic qualities: *sweet, salty, sour,* and
    bitter. Some taste buds are sensitive to only one of these qualities, while
    others respond to two, three, or all four of the qualities. Thus tastes are de-

    tected by the _____ _____, which contain receptors for the   taste buds

    qualities of _____, _____, _____, and _____.   sweet, salty, sour, bitter

16. The receptors for smell are located in the *olfactory epithelium,* a mem-
    brane in the nose. The receptors are sensitive to molecules mixed
    in the air. The impulses sent to the brain from the receptors in the

    _____ _____ determine the   olfactory epithelium
    odors we sense.

17. Since molecules must be mixed with air in order to be smelled, sub-
    stances that readily mix with air are detected most easily by the

    _____ _____.   olfactory epithelium

18. The skin possesses receptors for four stimuli: *pain, pressure, cold,* and
    warmth. In any single area there are usually more pain than pressure,
    more pressure than cold, and more cold than warmth receptors in the

    skin. Thus, in general, the most numerous receptors are for _____,   pain

    followed by _____, _____, and _____.   pressure, cold, warmth

19. Notice that although warmth is included among the four skin senses,

the feeling of hot is not. Ironically, we detect something as hot with the help of the cold receptors and a phenomenon called *paradoxical cold*. If a cold receptor is stimulated with heat in excess of 110 degrees Fahrenheit, the receptor sends a nervous impulse resulting in the sensation of

coldness, a phenomenon called _____ _____.

paradoxical cold

20. If both cold and warmth receptors are simultaneously touched with a stimulus of over 110 degrees, the combined result of warmth plus

_____ _____ is the sensation of hotness.

paradoxical cold

21. *Review*

  a. The sensory receptors for taste are the _____ _____ on the tongue and in the back of the mouth and in the throat. Four

  basic taste qualities are _____, _____, _____,

  and _____.

taste buds

sweet, salty, sour,

bitter

  b. The receptors for smell are located in the _____

  _____.

olfactory

epithelium

  c. Distributed throughout the skin are receptors for the senses of

  _____, _____, _____, and _____.

pain, pressure, cold,

warmth

  d. The feeling of hotness results from impulses from the warmth receptors plus those generated by the phenomenon of _____

  _____.

paradoxical

cold

22. The stimulus for hearing is the sound *wave*. The sound wave is an alternation of compression and expansion of the air. The rapid fluctuation of air pressure constitutes a sound _____.

wave

23. A diagram of a sound wave is presented in A of Figure 6–1. Sound waves vary from one another in three properties, the first of which is *frequency*. Frequency is the number of sound waves (or cycles) per second.

A

B

FIGURE 6–1

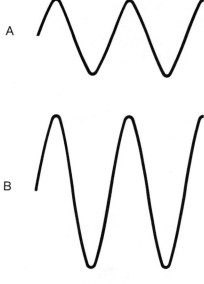

FIGURE 6–2

Part A of Figure 6–1 shows one cycle of a tone; part B shows the sound wave of a tone that has two cycles in the same length of time. Therefore, waves A and B differ in _____.   frequency

24. Differences in frequency result in the sensation of *pitch*. Middle C and high A represent a difference in _____, which we in-   frequency
terpret as a difference in their _____.   pitch

25. Sound waves may also differ in *amplitude*. Amplitude is the intensity of compression and expansion of the air and is indicated by the height of the wave in the diagram. Wave B in Figure 6–2 represents a tone that has twice the intensity of the one represented by wave A. The frequency of the waves remains the same, but waves A and B differ in

_____.   amplitude

26. Variation in amplitude results in variation in the sensation of *loud-ness*. Turning the stereo up and down changes the physical property of _____, which we hear as a difference in   amplitude
_____.   loudness

27. In addition to frequency and amplitude, sound waves vary in *complexity*. Simultaneously sounding the tones represented by A and B in Figure 6–1 would result in a third wave that relative to either A or B has more

_____.   complexity

28. The complexity of the sound wave determines the sensation of *timbre*. Roughly speaking, timbre means the characteristic quality of a tone. For example, middle C on a piano sounds quite different from the same note played on a trombone. The sound waves of the two tones

differ in _____, which we hear as a difference

in _____.

                        complexity

                        timbre

29. *Review*

    a. The three major properties of a sound wave are the number of
waves per second, or _____; the intensity of the
wave, or _____; and the intricacy of the wave,
known as _____.

                        frequency

                        amplitude

                        complexity

    b. Differences in frequency are heard as differences in _____,
differences in amplitude as differences in _____, and
differences in complexity as differences in _____.

                        pitch

                        loudness

                        timbre

30. The human ear is diagramed in Figure 6–3. The *outer ear* is composed
of the external structures of the ear and a canal that leads to the inner
portions of the ear. The external structures of the ear are part of the

    _____ _____.

                        outer ear

31. The first structure of the middle ear is the *eardrum,* a membrane that
vibrates when sound waves strike it. The outermost sound-sensitive

    structure of the middle ear is the _____.

                        eardrum

32. The eardrum is connected to the three *bones of the middle ear.* These
bones amplify vibrations from the eardrum and conduct them to the
inner ear. The conduction and amplification of sound in the middle ear

    is accomplished by the _____ ____ _____ _____

    _____.

                        bones of the middle

                        ear

33. Within the inner ear, the sound is received by the *oval window.* It
functions much like the eardrum except that the sound is conducted to

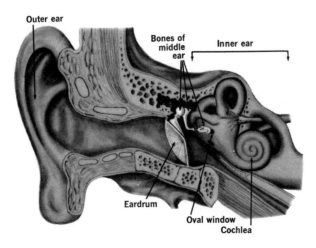

FIGURE 6–3

it by the bones of the middle ear rather than by sound waves in air. The

sound enters the inner ear at the _____ _____.   oval window

34. The sound waves are transmitted through the oval window to the
    cochlea, a large, bony structure shaped like a snail's shell. The principal

    structure of the inner ear is the _____.   cochlea

35. The space within the coiled cochlea is filled with fluid and is divided
    roughly in half by the *basilar membrane.* Sound waves transmitted from

    the oval window set up motions of the fluid that bend the _____   basilar

    _____, the tissue that divides the cochlea.   membrane

36. Located along the basilar membrane is the *organ of Corti,* a collection
    of hair cells that are stimulated when the basilar membrane bends. The
    hair cells then send impulses to the brain. Therefore, the receptors for

    hearing are the hair cells of the _____ ____ _____.   organ of Corti

37. *Review*

    a. Sound waves pass through the canal of the _____ _____   outer ear

    and strike the _____; they are then amplified and con-   eardrum

    ducted by the _____ ____ _____ _____ _____   bones of the middle ear

    to the _____ _____ of the inner ear.   oval window

    b. The sound waves transmitted from the oval window set up waves in

    the fluid of the _____, the principal structure of the   cochlea
    inner ear.

    c. The motion of the fluid bends a tissue within the cochlea called the

    _____ _____. This movement stimulates   basilar membrane

    the hair cells of the _____ ____ _____, which lie   organ of Corti
    along the membrane. The hair cells then send impulses to the brain
    that are interpreted as sound.

    d. Label the parts of the ear in the diagram below.

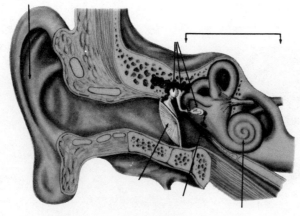

FIGURE 6-4

38. The stimulus for vision is the light wave, a pulsating form of electromagnetic energy. In a manner analogous to that of the sound wave, the light wave may vary in three different properties. The first is *wave length,* the distance between the peaks of the waves. The wave length of a light wave may be compared with the frequency of a sound wave. The rapidity with which the light energy pulsates determines its

_____ _____.   wave length

39. Second, the amount of energy in a light wave determines its *intensity.* The intensity of a light wave is parallel to the amplitude of a sound wave.

Therefore, the strength of a light wave is its _____.   intensity

40. Third, light waves vary in *complexity.* Like sound, light is often a mixture of several wave lengths, and the intricacy of that mixture determines

the light's _____.   complexity

41. Differences in these three physical characteristics of light are detected by our visual system. For example, differences in wave length are seen as differences in *hue,* the technical term for what is usually called color.

Differences in wave length are perceived as differences in _____.   hue

42. Differences in the intensity of light waves are seen as differences in the sensation of *brightness.* Generally, the more intensity a light source

has the more _____ it will appear to have.   brightness

43. Differences in the complexity of light waves produce the sensation of *saturation.* For example, some blues are blue and only blue—they are pure blue—but other blues are duller or grayer in color. A pure blue

has deep _____; a dull or gray-blue is lightly   saturation
saturated because white light is mixed in.

44. *Review*

    a. In contrast to a red light, a blue light has a different _____   wave

    _____, and thus we see it as having a different _____.   length, hue

    b. The strength or _____ of light determines the   intensity

    sensation of _____.   brightness

    c. The intricacy or _____ of the wave determines the   complexity

    sensation of _____.   saturation

45. The eye is a very complex sensory organ. Figure 6–5 is a diagram of the human eye. Over the front of the eye is the *cornea,* which is a transparent covering. When we put contact lenses on, we place them over

the _____.   cornea

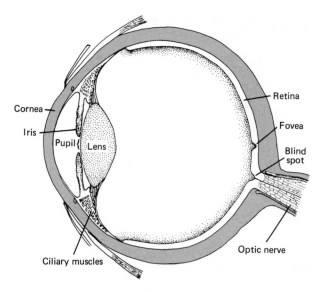

FIGURE 6–5

46. Just behind the cornea is the *iris*, the colored portion of the eye. The iris is like the diaphragm of a camera. Its muscles dilate and constrict according to the intensity of the light, permitting a relatively constant amount of light to enter the eye. What we see as the color of our eyes is

really the _____.   iris

47. The black spot in the middle of the eye is the *pupil*. This is the opening in the iris through which light passes into the inner portions of the eye.

When the illumination level is low, the size of the _____ in-   pupil
creases to admit the maximum amount of light.

48. Immediately behind the iris is the *lens*. The lens focuses the image on the light-sensitive portion of the inner eye. The visual image is kept in

focus by the _____.   lens

49. In contrast to the lens of a camera, which must be moved forward and back to adjust the focus on the film, the lens of the eye is stationary but is bulged or flattened by the *ciliary muscles* in order to maintain focus. Therefore, focusing on objects at various distances is accomplished by

changes in the shape of the lens produced by the _____   ciliary

_____.   muscles

50. *Review*
    a. When a light wave enters the eye it first passes through the trans-

    parent _____ and then through the "black" opening or   cornea

    _____, the size of which is determined by the dilation and   pupil

    constriction of the _____.   iris

b. The image is focused by the _____, which is bulged or flattened   lens

by the movement of the _____ _____.   ciliary muscles

51. The *retina* is the "film" of the eye. It covers the inside of the back of the eyeball and receives the light rays focused by the lens. The light-

sensitive receptor cells are found in the _____.   retina

52. There are two kinds of receptors in the retina. The *rods* are rather long and narrow receptors and do not respond to differences in hue but only to differences in intensity seen as black, white, and gray. At night, most

of our vision depends on the _____.   rods

53. The other receptor cells are the *cones.* They are somewhat thicker and more tapered than the rods and can respond to differences in hue. Color

vision is primarily a function of the _____.   cones

54. The rods and cones are not evenly distributed within the retina. There

are far fewer cones than _____, and while the rods tend to be   rods

found in the periphery of the eye, the _____ are more densely   cones
packed in the center of the retina.

55. The point of greatest concentration of cones is the *fovea;* in fact, the fovea contains only cones. The fovea is the most sensitive part of the retina; images that fall there are seen very clearly. Further, since cones are sensitive to differences in hue, color vision is best when the light

waves fall on the _____.   fovea

56. It appears that a chemical change is responsible for the stimulation of the vision receptors. The rods contain a substance called *visual purple,* which bleaches in the presence of light. It is this chemical change that causes the rods to respond. The cones contain substances similar to

_____ _____ that respond differentially to blue-   visual purple
violet, red, or green-yellow wave lengths.

57. Messages from the rods and cones of the eye travel to a bundle of nerve fibers called the *optic nerve,* which leads from the eye to the brain. The visual image then is interpreted in the rear portion of the brain.

The nerve link between the eye and the brain is the _____   optic

_____.   nerve

58. The point at which the optic nerve leaves the eye is the *blind spot.* Since the nerve fibers leaving the eye at this point are not sensitive to light, light waves falling on this area are not detected. Consequently,

this area is known as the _____ _____.   blind spot

59. *Review*

    a. Light striking the back of the eyeball falls on the _____,   retina
        which contains two general types of receptor cells.

    b. The long narrow cells that respond to intensities of light seen as

        black, white, and gray are _____, and the thicker, more tapered   rods

        cells sensitive to differences in hue are _____. The cones are   cones

        most densely packed in the _____ of the eye.   fovea

    c. A chemical change, for example, the bleaching of _____   visual

        _____ in the rods, causes the receptor cells to send their   purple
        messages to the brain.

    d. The bundle of nerve fibers that leads from the eye to the brain is the

        _____ _____. The point at which it leaves the eye   optic nerve

        constitutes the _____ _____.   blind spot

    e. Label the parts of the eye in the diagram below.

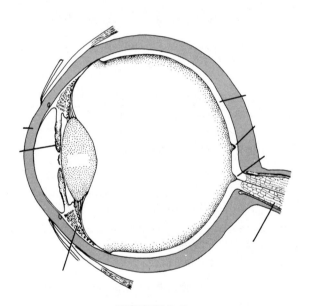

FIGURE 6–6

60. The receptors for the sense of equilibrium are in the *semicircular canals*
    located in the inner ear. (You may refer to the diagram of the ear in
    Figure 6–3. The semicircular canals are the three loops above the
    cochlea.) A fluid, following the laws of gravity, moves about in these
    canals as a function of the orientation of our heads. Therefore, as we tilt
    our heads, the fluid is set in motion, stimulating certain hair cells within

    the _____ _____ that send im-   semicircular canals
    pulses to the brain. It is these messages that are interpreted as our sense
    of equilibrium.

self-test

_____ 1. Any form of energy capable of exciting the nervous system is a
a. receptor
b. threshold
c. stimulus
d. percept

_____ 2. A specialized nerve ending capable of responding to a stimulus is a
a. threshold
b. limen
c. receptor
d. j.n.d.

_____ 3. The point at which a stimulus is intense enough to be detected half the time is called the
a. absolute threshold
b. subliminal level
c. difference limen
d. j.n.d.

_____ 4. The proposition that in order to detect a difference in stimulation the stimulus must be increased a constant percentage of its initial intensity is called
a. the concept of absolute limen
b. Weber's Law
c. sensory adaptation
d. threshold constancies

_____ 5. Our taste receptors can detect
a. sweet and bitter
b. sour and salty
c. sweet, sour, tangy, and bitter
d. sweet, salty, bitter, sour

_____ 6. The membrane containing the receptors for smell is the
a. mucosa
b. olfactory epithelium
c. basilar membrane
d. organ of Corti

_____ 7. The two-point threshold for the sense of pressure is measured by an
a. EEG
b. esthesiometer
c. audiometer
d. oscilloscope

_____ 8. When we experience paradoxical cold
a. the warmth receptors interpret a warm stimulus as cold
b. a warm stimulus feels cold if a cold stimulus is nearby
c. the cold receptors interpret a very warm stimulus as cold
d. a cold stimulus feels cold even though a very hot stimulus is nearby

_____ 9. The skin-mapping technique has indicated the possibility that
a. pressure and cold receptors are the same cells
b. there are about the same number of pressure and pain receptors in a given area of the skin
c. the sensation of cold and warmth comes from the same cell
d. pressure, pain, cold, and warmth stimuli are generally received by different receptors

10. Most of our psychological experiences of sound are a function of the three physical properties of sound waves listed on the left, namely _frequency, amplitude,_ and _complexity._ On the right are eleven terms or phrases. Next to each item in the right-hand list, write the letter of the physical attribute that is most closely related to it.

a. frequency
b. amplitude
c. complexity

1. intensity _____
2. pitch _____
3. timbre _____
4. overtone _____
5. height of sound wave _____

6. middle C _____
7. rapidity
   of cycle _____
8. decibel _____
9. several
   frequencies
   simultaneously _____
10. loudness _____
11. sound waves
    per second _____

11. divides cochlea
    into two
    chambers _____

11. On the left is a list of the basic structures of the ear. On the right is a list of statements about these structures. Write the letter of the structure most closely associated with each statement in the blank provided.

a. basilar
   membrane
b. bones of
   the middle
   ear
c. eardrum
d. organ of
   Corti
e. cochlea
f. oval
   window

1. houses basilar
   membrane _____
2. transmit sound
   wave from
   eardrum to
   oval window _____
3. stimulation of
   this structure
   establishes
   nervous
   impulse _____
4. transmits
   sound wave
   from middle to
   inner ear _____
5. shaped like a
   snail's shell _____
6. amplify sound _____
7. outermost
   sound-sensitive
   structure _____
8. made up of
   hair cells _____
9. receives sound
   wave from
   bones of the
   middle ear _____
10. largest
    structure in
    inner ear _____

_____12. The traveling wave theory suggests that the
   a. basilar membrane acts like a harp
   b. hair cells of the organ of Corti vibrate sympathetically with sounds
   c. entire basilar membrane moves with the sound but some parts move more than others, depending on the frequency
   d. oval window sets up a miniature sound wave within the cochlea that stimulates the eardrum

13. On the left is a list of the important components of the eye. On the right is a list of statements and concepts related to these components. Next to each item in the right-hand list, write the letter of the component most closely associated with it.

a. fovea
b. retina
c. visual
   purple
d. pupil
e. optic
   nerve
f. rods
g. ciliary
   muscles
h. iris
i. lens
j. cones

1. most sensitive
   area of retina _____
2. opening for
   light to enter _____
3. chemical pos-
   sessed by rods _____
4. analogous to
   photographic
   film _____
5. bleached by
   light _____
6. changes shape
   in accord with
   distance of
   object to be
   focused _____
7. analogous to
   diaphragm of a
   camera _____
8. area of high
   concentration
   of cones _____
9. most numerous
   type of
   receptor _____

10. eye color _____
11. contains rods and cones _____
12. leads from eye toward brain _____
13. causes blind spot _____
14. focuses light rays _____
15. regulates amount of light falling on retina _____
16. responsible for color vision _____
17. changes shape of lens _____
18. black-and-white receptors _____

_____14. Frequency is to pitch as wave length is to
a. intensity
b. saturation
c. hue
d. light energy

_____15. The brightness of a particular hue depends on the light wave's
a. wave length
b. frequency
c. intensity
d. intensity and wave length

_____16. The word most closely associated with saturation is
a. brightness
b. purity
c. afterimages
d. amplitude

_____17. A hue mixed with a complementary hue produces
a. gray

b. the opposite color
c. the color on the edge of the color circle midway between the two
d. a color that makes the original hue more vivid

_____18. Visual images usually do not fade away through the process of adaptation because
a. our eyes are making 30 to 100 tiny movements every second
b. rods and cones adapt so slowly to constant stimulation that it is hardly noticeable
c. there are so many rods and cones that they do not appear to adapt
d. our attention shifts rapidly over a visual display

_____19. The receptors found in the muscles, tendons, and joints all serve the sense of
a. balance
b. bodily movement
c. pressure
d. vestibular orientation

_____20. The vestibule and the semicircular canals are in the
a. back of the retina
b. joints of our bones
c. muscle layers
d. inner ear

Key to Self-Test

1. (c); 2. (c); 3. (a); 4. (b); 5. (d); 6. (b); 7. (b); 8. (c); 9. (d); 10. (b, a, c, c, b, a, a, b, c, b, a); 11. (e, b, d, f, e, b, c, d, f, e, a); 12. (c); 13. (a, d, c, b, c, i, h, a, f, h, b, e, e, i, h, j, g, f); 14. (c); 15. (d); 16. (b); 17. (a); 18. (a); 19. (b); 20. (d)

exercises

I. Many of our sensations depend on prior sensory experience and adaptation. This fact can be demonstrated by putting one hand in cold water and the other in hot water for a few minutes. Then put both hands into lukewarm water. For the hand adapted to the cold temperature the lukewarm water will feel warm, maybe even hot, while the hand adapted to hot water may sense the lukewarm temperature as being quite cool. Discuss the following questions in view of this principle.

Questions

1. Why does a baseball player swing a bat weighted with lead before facing the pitcher?
2. Why do Navy personnel sometimes wear dark red goggles for a half-hour before going out on deck for the night watch? Why not use yellow rather than red?

II. Describe and explain how we see differences in hue, brightness, and saturation by outlining the various structures of the visual system and their functions in producing these sensations.

III. By using the tests in Plate V in Chapter 6 of your text, try to locate a person who is color blind. (If you are color blind, have another student do this exercise with you.) You are more likely to find one among your male friends, since approximately 7 percent of males but only .1 percent of females have some form of color deficiency. After you have located such a person, attempt to ascertain the nature of his defect by showing him objects of different hues, such as colored pencils, pieces of colored paper, and so forth—but not objects whose color he might be able to name correctly from other clues (for instance, grass is usually green). Determine if he is red-green, blue-yellow, or totally color blind. If he is red-green blind, for example, what color does he call green or red objects? Does he say they are shades of gray or some other color such as brown or blue? How might you explain the fact that a red object may look orange, yellow, or brown but not gray? How well does the subject function in his environment despite his deficiency? What noncolor clues does he use to determine colors that he cannot see (as, for example, a stoplight)?

CHAPTER 7 PERCEPTION

programed unit

1. *Perception* is the process through which we become aware of our environment by organizing and interpreting the evidence of our senses. When we "see" a dog we have organized the pattern of light and interpreted it as being a given thing, namely a dog. Thus, "seeing a dog"

   constitutes a _____.   perception

2. Perceptions differ from sensations. Although our sensory systems organize stimuli to a limited extent, most of the organization and interpretation of sensory information belongs in the realm of _____.   perception

3. Sometimes our interpretation of sensory information is not precisely the same as the actual facts. For example, *stroboscopic motion* is the apparent movement produced by a rapid succession of images that are actually stationary. A movie is really composed of a series of still pictures flashed on the screen in rapid succession. Thus, the movement

   we perceive on the screen is _____   stroboscopic

   _____.   motion

4. The simplest type of stroboscopic motion is known as the *phi phenomenon*. If three lights are in a line and each flashes in sequence, you might perceive a spot of light moving from left to right across your field of vision rather than three separate flashes of light. Apparent movement produced by the flashing of stationary lights in sequence illustrates the

   simplest type of _____ _____,   stroboscopic motion

   known as the _____ _____.   phi phenomenon

5. Another type of apparent movement is the *gamma phenomenon*. A dim light appears smaller than a brighter light of the same size. Furthermore, as a light gets brighter it appears to move closer to the observer. The apparent shift in size and distance as a function of the brightness of

   a light is called the _____ _____.   gamma phenomenon

6. Sometimes a single stationary light or object will be perceived as moving in a phenomenon known as the *autokinetic illusion*. If a person in a dark room is asked to look at a stationary pinpoint of light, he may report that the spot of light moves up and down and around, even though the light is actually perfectly still. This apparent movement of a single stationary light is called the _____ _____.

autokinetic

illusion

7. *Review*
   a. The process through which we become aware of our environment by organizing and interpreting sensory evidence is called _____.

perception

   b. Occasionally our perceptions of an event do not correspond to the actual situation. For example, sometimes we perceive things as moving although they are actually stationary. The apparent movement produced by a rapid succession of stationary images is called _____ _____, the simplest case of which is the _____ _____.

stroboscopic motion

phi phenomenon

   c. A second type of apparent movement, involving the perception of changes in the size and distance of a fixed light that only changes in brightness, is the _____ _____.

gamma phenomenon

   d. Finally, when a person perceives a stationary pinpoint of light in an otherwise dark room as moving, he is experiencing the _____ _____.

autokinetic illusion

8. A key factor in perception is *selection*. Our senses can detect an enormous variety of sensory information; were we to be constantly aware of all stimuli that they can detect, the bombardment of sensory information would be overwhelming. Instead we select the stimuli to which we will pay attention. We do not constantly notice the ticking of a clock, although if we stop to concentrate on it we can certainly hear it. Therefore, the perceptual system filters the incoming sensory information according to the process of _____.

selection

9. Another fundamental factor in perception is *organization*. Without this tendency to organize stimuli, we would perceive the world as a mass of hopelessly disjointed sensory patterns. Grouping certain patterns together and distinguishing them from other stimulus complexes constitutes perceptual _____.

organization

10. These two processes of perception, _____ and _____, are influenced by a wide variety of circumstances. The factors that affect selection will be considered first, followed by those that influence organization.

selection

organization

11. That which we selectively attend to is frequently determined by the

characteristics of the stimulus and our experience with it. For example, we may soon quit paying attention to a steady and continuous stimulus. However, we may immediately pay attention to the stimulus again if it undergoes a *change*. The grandfather clock that ticks in the living room is seldom noticed unless it stops. We may be aware of the presence of a watch for a brief time after acquiring a new watchband because of

the factor of a _____ in stimulation.   change

12. One attention-compelling form of change is *movement*. A deer quietly grazing in a thicket may not even be noticed, but when it runs away,

our attention will certainly be attracted because of its _____.   movement

13. Another form of change is *contrast*. Something that stands out in marked relief against its background gains attention because of its

_____.   contrast

14. Sometimes these two stimulus characteristics work together. For example, a few states encourage drivers to turn on their headlights during the day on major holidays. Traffic officials feel that this keeps drivers alert because the sight of headlights during the day represents a

_____ from what motorists are accustomed to seeing, and   change

the brightness of the lights represents a _____ with   contrast
the surrounding stimuli.

15. Sometimes *repetition* makes us more attentive to a stimulus. Frequently a young child will love to watch a TV commercial that has become familiar to him through repetition. Thus, although with too much familiarity we may become bored with a stimulus, sometimes an event may be made more outstanding and gain our attention through

_____.   repetition

16. *Size* is also a stimulus characteristic that affects selection. Other factors being equal, a large object is more likely to attract our attention than a small one. Newspapers capitalize on this fact by giving major stories large headlines, thus directing our attention by the differential use of

_____.   size

17. A final factor in selection of stimuli is *intensity*. Everything else being equal, the louder of two tones or the brighter of two lights will more

likely attract our attention because of its greater _____.   intensity

18. *Review*
   a. A principal function of our perceptual system is to weed out stimuli

   for attention by the process of _____.   selection
   b. Several stimulus characteristics influence this selection. A continuous or repeated stimulus eventually goes unnoticed, but a sudden al-

teration in that stimulus does recruit attention because of the

_____.   *change*

   c. There are several specific types of change that attract attention. A running herd of horses attracts more attention than a quietly

grazing herd because of its _____. Black-on-white   *movement*
lettering attracts more attention than dark gray on lighter gray be-

cause of its greater _____.   *contrast*

   d. Stimuli made familiar through _____ may   *repetition*
command our attention; large objects tend to be selected over smaller

ones because of their _____; and loud sounds attract more   *size*

attention than soft sounds because of their _____.   *intensity*

19. *Organization* as well as selection influences the way we perceive stimuli. We do not see mere blotches of light or random lines and contours, but rather trees, houses, people, and so on, because of our tendency

toward _____ of stimulus information in   *organization*
our perceptions.

20. One organizational tendency is to separate *figure* and *ground*. Whenever we perceive an object, we distinguish it from its background. The object

represents a _____ and its setting is called the _____.   *figure, ground*

21. Our tendency to organize sensations into figure and ground is so pervasive that we seldom are aware of this perceptual trait until we encounter a stimulus such as the one illustrated below. Stop for a moment and look at it. One sees either a goblet or two faces, or one vacillates between seeing first the goblet and then the faces. Note that you cannot see both at the same time because either you view the white portion as

_____ and the black as _____, or the reverse.   *figure, ground*

FIGURE 7–1

22. The dividing line that separates figure from ground is called the *contour*. In Figure 7–1, the black edge (or the white edge, depending on how you view the stimulus) is the _____.

contour

23. Another organizational tendency is *closure,* the process whereby we perceive a figure as complete even if parts of the contour are missing. A circle with a broken circumference may still be perceived as a "circle" because of _____.

closure

24. In addition to figure and ground and closure, *continuity* determines the way we organize our sensations. We tend to perceive continuous lines and patterns. Consider Figure 7–2:

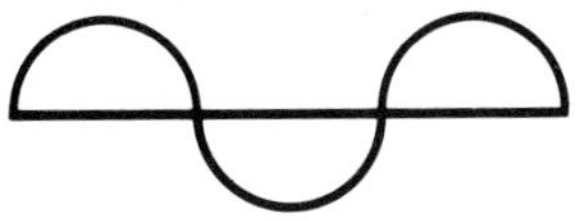

FIGURE 7–2

Most people see this as two lines, one straight and one wavy, rather than as a series of semicircles. This is because the lines have more _____ than do the semicircles.

continuity

25. Furthermore, we organize by grouping objects on the basis of their *proximity;* that is, we make patterns of stimuli that are close together. The display

x y   w z

is seen most often as two pairs of letters, not as four letters, because of the factor of _____.

proximity

26. We also make patterns of stimuli that have *similarity.* The grouping

x x y y

is seen as two pairs of letters rather than as a string of four letters because of _____.

similarity

27. Lastly, we organize stimuli on the basis of *common movement.* A snake motionless in the grass is difficult to see, but when it moves we perceptually group all the moving stimuli together and they become an object — the snake — because of the factor of _____ _____.

common

movement

28. *Review*
   a. In addition to selecting stimuli to which we will attend, our perceptual system orders our sensory world by _____.

organization

   b. In order to see objects as distinct from their surroundings, we organize our sensations into _____ and _____,   figure, ground

which are separated by a _____.   contour

c. We perceive an object as complete even if parts are missing through

the process of _____.   closure

d. We perceive the drawing in Figure 7–2 as two lines rather than as a series of semicircles because of the organizational factor of

_____.   continuity

e. We tend to make patterns of stimuli that are close together. That

is, we organize them on the basis of _____.   proximity

f. We also tend to make patterns of stimuli that share common charac-

teristics, or have _____.   similarity

g. Lastly, stimuli that move together are organized into a pattern be-

cause of the perceptual factor of _____ _____.   common movement

29. One entire group of organizational tendencies is referred to as *perceptual constancy*. The fact that various qualities of objects are seen as constant even though we view the objects from a different angle, see them from a different distance, or observe them in a different context

defines the concept of _____ _____.   perceptual constancy

30. One such perceptual constancy is *shape constancy*. When a rectangular window is viewed from different angles, the actual image of the window on the eye may be a trapezoid or parallelogram, yet the window is still

perceived as rectangular because of _____ _____.   shape constancy

31. *Brightness constancy* is the tendency to see objects according to their known brightness rather than their actual physical brightness. A highly polished black shoe shining brightly in the sun may reflect just as much light as a white handbag in the shade, but we see the latter as being

brighter as a result of _____ _____.   brightness constancy

32. There is also *color constancy*. In one experiment, pieces of gray paper were cut into the forms of various fruits, mounted on blue-green backgrounds, and covered with screens. All the papers should have looked the same color. However, the subjects perceived the papers as having the colors of the fruits they represented, illustrating the

tendency toward _____ _____.   color constancy

33. Another perceptual constancy is *location constancy*. When we shake our heads back and forth, the objects around us do not appear to whirl by as our sensations might suggest. The objects appear to remain in place

because of _____ _____.   location constancy

34. *Size constancy* is vital to our perceptual functioning. Although a mouse seen at a distance of 1 foot covers more of the visual field than a man

seen at a distance of 100 yards, the man will still be perceived as bigger

because of our tendency toward _____ _____.   size constancy

35. *Review*

    a. The tendency to perceive objects as constant and unchanging
       even though the images of them that reach our senses vary is called

       _____ _____.   perceptual constancy

    b. Seeing a plate as circular regardless of the viewing angle illustrates

       _____ _____. Seeing a dim white circle   shape constancy
       as brighter than an intensely illuminated gray circle demonstrates

       _____ _____.   brightness constancy

    c. Seeing a lemon as yellow regardless of the lighting conditions il-

       lustrates _____ _____; perceiving the   color constancy

       position of objects as unvarying constitutes _____   location

       _____; and maintaining the height relationships   constancy
       between an elephant and a dog regardless of the actual height of the

       visual image illustrates _____ _____.   size constancy

36. Frequently we are required to make judgments of distance or depth.
    One clue in determining the distance of an object is its *perceived size.*
    A basketball is judged to be nearer to us the larger it appears. Even
    when two similar objects are actually the same distance away, with
    no other clues available, the bigger object will appear closer because

    of the influence of _____ _____ on distance   perceived size
    perception.

37. Another clue in determining distance is *binocular vision.* Binocular
    vision refers to the fact that, since our eyes are approximately 2½ inches
    apart, one eye does not see precisely the same image as the other. The

    difference between the two images that is due to _____   binocular

    _____ helps us judge distance.   vision

38. To illustrate, hold your finger about 6 inches from your nose and focus
    on a distant object. Alternately close one eye and then the other. Your
    finger appears to jump with respect to the distant object. However, it
    jumps less if you hold it at arm's length rather than at 6 inches. This
    difference is one of the clues to determining distance and derives from

    having _____ _____.   binocular vision

39. A more obvious clue to distance is *interposition.* Simply stated, near
    objects stand between our eyes and more distant objects. The fact
    that a near object blocks from view part of a more distant object is

    termed _____.   interposition

40. Another set of clues to distance involves the rules of *perspective*. For centuries, artists have been able to give the impression of distance and three dimensions on a flat surface by using the rules of _____.

perspective

41. There are three kinds of perspective. One is *linear perspective*, the fact that parallel lines seem to draw closer as they recede into the distance. Railroad tracks that appear to converge in the distance are a classic example of _____ _____.

linear perspective

42. The second kind, *aerial perspective*, refers to the fact that distant objects, because they are seen through air that is usually somewhat hazy, appear less distinct and less brilliant in color than nearby objects. The relative distances of skyscrapers or mountains can often be determined on the basis of _____ _____.

aerial perspective

43. The third kind of perspective is *gradient of texture*, the fact that the perceived texture of objects changes with their distance from the viewer. Lie down in the grass and notice that each blade close to you is distinct and the lawn nearby has a coarse and sharp texture; farther away, the detail is less clear and the texture appears to be finer. This difference in perceived texture with distance represents the _____ _____ _____.

gradient
of texture

44. Another aid in the judgment of distance and especially of height and depth is *motion parallax*, the fact that when we move our heads, near objects cross our field of vision more rapidly than objects that are farther away. Look across the room and select a near and a far vertically oriented object. Now walk sideways and notice that the nearer object moves across the visual field more rapidly than the distant object, illustrating the concept of _____ _____.

motion parallax

45. *Review*
    a. Several factors influence our perception of distance and depth. The larger of two similar objects will be judged nearer because of the principle of _____ _____.

    perceived size

    b. Another clue to distance is the fact that our two eyes do not see precisely the same image, called _____ _____.

    binocular vision

    c. The fact that a near object may obscure part of a more distant object, called _____, also influences distance perception.

    interposition

    d. Railroad tracks that appear to converge in the distance and faraway objects that seem hazier than near objects illustrate _____ and _____ _____.

    linear
    aerial perspective

    e. The difference in the perceived texture of objects with distance is known as the _____ _____ _____.

    gradient of texture

f. The fact that near objects move across our visual field more rapid-

ly than objects that are farther away, called _____   motion

_____, offers a further clue to distance and especially   parallax

to height and depth.

self-test

_____ 1. Perception is the process through which we become aware of
  a. the stimuli impinging on us
  b. our environment by organizing and interpreting our sense data
  c. the stimuli around us by attending differentially to certain aspects of the environment
  d. our environment by labeling and categorizing our feelings

_____ 2. Motion pictures are based on
  a. the gamma phenomenon
  b. the principle of the illusory circle
  c. the autokinetic illusion
  d. stroboscopic motion

_____ 3. The phi phenomenon is frequently used as an element of advertising signs because it
  a. is pleasing to look at
  b. has smooth contours
  c. captures our attention
  d. has hidden persuaders

_____ 4. A type of perceived movement that plagues pilots, in which a stationary light appears to move, is called the
  a. gamma phenomenon
  b. phi phenomenon
  c. autokinetic illusion
  d. illusory circle

_____ 5. Which of the following is *not* a factor in the selection of stimuli?
  a. perceptual constancy
  b. change
  c. intensity
  d. repetition

_____ 6. Seeing a chair in a living room setting illustrates the concept of
  a. shadowing
  b. contrast
  c. closure
  d. figure-ground

_____ 7. The fact that we can see form in a sketch of an object that is composed only of dots illustrates the concept of
  a. contrast
  b. closure
  c. contour
  d. figure-ground

_____ 8. The fact that the display *vw xy* is seen as two pairs illustrates the concept of
  a. contrast
  b. similarity
  c. proximity
  d. closure

_____ 9. Perceiving a book lying on a table as being rectangular though seen from an oblique angle is an example of
  a. contrast
  b. perceptual constancy
  c. closure
  d. proximity

_____10. Perceptual constancies are
  a. illusions in which we perceive something that does not correspond to the sensory information
  b. confusing to an individual rather than helping him determine what really exists
  c. likely inborn and not subject to learning
  d. an aid in perceiving a stable and consistent world

_____11. Wearing lenses that invert the visual field results in
  a. perceptual disorganization for several months, after which the world turns right side up
  b. permanent disorganization
  c. almost no disorganization at all
  d. disorganization at first, after which the person is gradually able to function in the strange environment

_____12. The phenomena that occur when we wear a pseudophone or inverted lenses for a length of time demonstrate our tendency to establish
  a. location constancy
  b. shape constancy
  c. interposition
  d. motion parallax

_____13. Location constancy
  a. is inborn
  b. cannot be modified by experience
  c. can be developed by simply watching stimulus events and observing the location of objects
  d. is developed in part by moving around one's environment and learning to combine perception and motor coordination

_____14. Which is *not* a clue used in perceiving distance?
  a. aerial perspective
  b. binocular vision
  c. continuity
  d. interposition

_____15. The fact that distant objects look hazy is embodied in the principle of
  a. interposition
  b. shadowing
  c. aerial perspective
  d. linear perspective

_____16. Apparently, the essential clue to depth perception on the "visual cliff" is
  a. binocular vision
  b. aerial perspective
  c. motion parallax
  d. interposition

_____17. When visual evidence conflicts with the evidence of touch, we
  a. tend to believe our eyes
  b. are unable to attain a clear-cut perception
  c. compromise between the two impressions
  d. tend to believe the sense of touch

_____18. In an experiment with rats, ability to discriminate between triangles and squares was found to depend on having grown up in an environment that contained
  a. curves
  b. circles
  c. angles
  d. any type of geometric figure

_____19. The experiment in which one kitten could freely move about a visual environment while another kitten was transported through the same environment in a "gondola" demonstrated that
  a. movement is necessary for the adequate development of motor skills
  b. movement in a visual environment is necessary for the development of normal visual behavior
  c. visual stimuli are necessary for the adequate development of motor skills
  d. the kitten in the gondola paid no attention to the visual stimuli

_____20. Being "forewarned" about the personality of an individual one is about to meet creates
  a. learning sets
  b. perceptual expectations
  c. interposition
  d. perceptual constancies

Key to Self-Test

1. (b); 2. (d); 3. (c); 4. (c); 5. (a); 6. (d); 7. (b); 8. (c); 9. (b); 10. (d); 11. (d); 12. (a); 13. (d); 14. (c); 15. (c); 16. (c); 17. (a); 18. (c); 19. (b); 20. (b)

exercises

Below is an old studio photograph of Humphrey Bogart that contains many objects. Find two subjects; ask the first to look at the picture for thirty seconds and then give him one minute to write down as many objects in the picture as he can remember. Use the same procedure for the second subject except limit his examination of the picture to five seconds.

I. Compare the lists of all the objects remembered under each of the two conditions. Did some objects seem easier to remember than others? What objects did the five-second subject recall? From what you know about selection as a function of perception and the factors governing memory, can you explain why these objects should be at-tended to and remembered more easily than others? Did the thirty-second subject also tend to recall these same objects? What was the difference between the items remembered by the two subjects? Do you think the principles of perception functioned more obviously for the five-second subject than for the thirty-second subject? Why?

II. Pool your findings with several of your classmates. Record the number of objects remembered by each of the subjects tested under each of the two conditions. Add these scores and obtain the average for each group. Were there differences in the average number of objects remembered by the subjects who were allowed thirty seconds versus those allowed five? Why?

FIGURE 7–3

CHAPTER 8 HEREDITY, GLANDS, AND NERVOUS SYSTEM

programed unit

1. The determinants of human heredity are found in twenty-three pairs of *chromosomes* in every body cell. Characteristics of parents are transmitted to their offspring through the _____.

   chromosomes

2. Although the cells of the body contain twenty-three pairs of chromosomes, the sex cells, sperm and egg, do not have pairs but twenty-three single chromosomes. During fertilization the twenty-three chromosomes of the father are matched with those of the mother, resulting in a cell with a new combination of twenty-three pairs of _____.

   chromosomes

3. Chromosomes are composed of a large number of *genes.* Each of the father's sperm cells and each egg from the mother contains a different pattern of genes. When a sperm and an egg cell meet, just one of an uncountable number of possible combinations takes place. Consequently, the great variety of traits, even within a single family, is a result of the many possible combinations of _____.

   genes

4. Genes are composed of a chemical called DNA. The pattern of atoms within the genes is believed to constitute a "code" that directs the development of the body and determines our characteristics. Therefore, our heredity depends on the many _____ that make up the

   genes

   twenty-three _____ of the sex cells.

   chromosomes

5. Each pair of genes (one on each paired chromosome), alone or in combination with other genes, contributes to the determination of a trait. Suppose, however, one gene is for blue eyes and another for brown. What trait results? It happens that the gene for brown eyes is *dominant.* Therefore, if a child inherits one gene for blue and one for brown eyes, he will have brown eyes because the gene for brown is _____.

   dominant

6. The gene for blue eyes is *recessive*. The effects of a recessive gene always tend to be suppressed by the dominant gene. Therefore, in a brown-blue pairing the gene for blue is suppressed because it is

_____.   recessive

7. If Br represents the gene for brown eyes and Bl symbolizes blue, then the pairings of Br-Br, Br-Bl, and Bl-Br will all result in brown eye

color because the gene for brown is _____. Only a   dominant
Bl-Bl combination will result in blue eyes, because in order to produce

blue both _____ genes must be present.   recessive

8. *Review*
   a. The sex cells of each parent have twenty-three _____   chromosomes
      that pair up during fertilization.
   b. Every chromosome is composed of many smaller structures called

      _____, the chemical and atomic structure of which consti-   genes
      tutes a code for transmitting traits from parents to child.
   c. A gene that produces its trait regardless of the nature of the other

      gene in the pair is _____. A gene whose effects are   dominant

      suppressed is _____.   recessive

9. The *endocrine glands* secrete chemicals directly into the blood stream. They are sometimes called "ductless glands" because they possess no ducts for the delivery of their substances. Glands without ducts that secrete their products directly into the blood stream are called

   _____ glands.   endocrine

10. Salivary glands are indeed glands, but they have ducts to the surface of the mouth. Therefore, they are not ductless and they do not empty their products directly into the blood stream. Thus, salivary glands are

   not _____ glands.   endocrine

11. The chemical product of an endocrine gland is a *hormone*. Hormone means "activator"; the hormones activate and control many kinds of bodily functions and behavior. The secretion of an endocrine gland is a

   _____.   hormone

12. Figure 8–1 diagrams the location of seven major endocrine glands of the human body. The master gland is the *pituitary*. This gland secretes hormones that govern growth, cause sexual development at puberty, and regulate other endocrine glands. The master gland, which secretes hormones that have a profound effect on the life process, is the

   _____.   pituitary

13. The *thyroid* regulates metabolism, which is the never-ending process

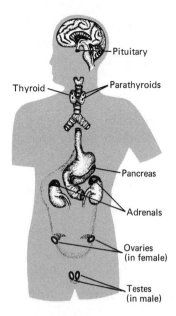

FIGURE 8–1

by which the cells inside the body convert food into energy or proto-
plasm. General activity level, body weight, and susceptibility to fatigue
are all influenced by the _____.

thyroid

14. The *parathyroids* regulate the balance of calcium and phosphorus in
the blood, thus maintaining a normal state of excitability of the nervous system. The glands that lie around the thyroid gland are the

_____.

parathyroids

15. Thus, in the region of the head and throat there are three major endocrine glands. The master gland is the _____. General

pituitary

metabolism is regulated by the _____, and the level of

thyroid

excitability of the nervous system is kept in balance by the _____.

parathyroids

16. Located in the trunk of the body below the stomach is the *pancreas,*
which produces hormones that control the level of sugar in the blood.
Since blood sugar is burned by the body, the body's available source

of energy is controlled by the _____.

pancreas

17. The pancreas secretes one of the best-known hormones, *insulin.* It is
insulin that controls the amount of sugar in the blood. An underactive
pancreas results in the disease called diabetes. Diabetics can control

their blood sugar by taking various amounts of _____ in

insulin

order to compensate for an underactive _____.

pancreas

18. There are two *adrenal* glands, each secreting hormones that govern a

variety of functions. In Figure 8–1 the glands lying on top of the kidneys

are the _____ glands.   adrenal

19. Two hormones produced by the adrenal medulla, or inner part of the
adrenals, are *adrenalin* and *noradrenalin*. These two chemicals affect
heart rate, blood pressure, and emergency outputs of blood sugar. Since
these hormones frequently stimulate the organism in preparation for

action of some kind, two powerful stimulants are _____   adrenalin

and _____.   noradrenalin

20. The outer portion of the adrenals, the adrenal cortex, produces a number of essential hormones called *steroids*. Steroids help maintain a
suitable salt balance in the body and convert body proteins into sugar

to supply energy. Death would ensue shortly without _____.   steroids

21. The glands situated on top of the kidneys are the _____.   adrenals
Heart rate, blood pressure, and the emergency supply of blood sugar

are regulated by the hormones _____ and   adrenalin

_____; salt balance and the conversion of   noradrenalin

protein to sugar are managed by _____.   steroids

22. Hormones secreted by the *ovaries* and *testes,* the last group of endocrine
glands, control the development of secondary sex characteristics. The
growth of the breasts and regulation of the menstrual cycle are con-

trolled by the _____; the growth of a beard and the deepen-   ovaries

ing of the voice are governed by the _____.   testes

23. *Review*
   a. Ductless, or _____, glands produce chemicals   endocrine

      known as _____.   hormones

   b. The master gland of the body is the _____.   pituitary

   c. Located in the throat and governing metabolism is the _____, thyroid

      and around it are the _____, which help   parathyroids
      maintain a normal state of excitability of the nervous system.
   d. Determining the blood sugar level is the function of the hormone

      _____, which is secreted by the _____.   insulin, pancreas

   e. Located on top of the kidneys, the _____ regulate   adrenals
      heart rate, blood pressure, and emergency sources of blood sugar by

      secreting _____ and _____;   adrenalin, noradrenalin
      the salt balance in the blood and the conversion of protein to sugar

      are influenced by the adrenal hormones called _____.   steroids

f. Secondary sex characteristics are governed by the _____   ovaries

in the female and the _____ in the male.   testes

g. Figure 8–2 is a duplicate of Figure 8–1 but without the labels. Identify each endocrine gland and list its functions without referring to the previous drawing.

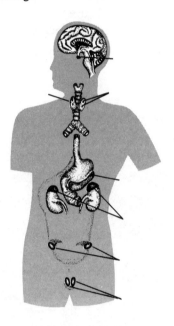

FIGURE 8–2

24. The basic unit of the nervous system is the *neuron,* or nerve cell, which is diagramed in Figure 8–3. It may vary in length from a small fraction

of an inch to several feet. An individual nerve cell is called a _____.   neuron

25. The widest portion of the neuron is the *cell body.* Its function is to govern the metabolism, or energy needs, of the cell. The nutritional

requirements of the nerve cell are managed by its _____   cell

_____.   body

26. The *dendrites* are located at one end of the neuron. When stimulated, the dendrites fire a nervous impulse to the other end of the neuron. The branching network that receives stimulation and starts a nervous impulse that travels the length of the neuron is made up of the

_____.   dendrites

27. At the opposite end of the neuron is the *axon.* At this end the impulse stimulates another neuron, a muscle, or a gland. The "sending" end of

a neuron is its _____.   axon

28. Many axons are surrounded by a *myelin sheath,* which improves the transmission of the nervous impulse. The nervous impulse travels

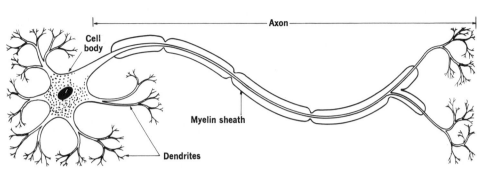

FIGURE 8–3

almost 100 times faster if the neuron has a _____   myelin

_____ than if it does not.   sheath

29. *Review*
    a. The basic unit of the nervous system is the _____.   neuron

    b. When an impulse arrives at a neuron it is received by the_____.   dendrites

    c. Next the impulse is transmitted through the _____ _____,   cell body
    which governs the cell's metabolism.

    d. It travels on through the _____, which then sends the impulse   axon
    to another neuron, a muscle, or a gland.

    e. The impulse travels more rapidly if the neuron has a _____   myelin

    _____.   sheath

30. The nervous *impulse* is a traveling change in the electrochemical nature
    of the neuron. Although it is tempting to think of it as an electrical
    pulse traveling along a fiber, this is only a vague analogy to the actual

    character of the nervous _____.   impulse

31. The *synapse* is the "junction" between two neurons where the impulse
    is transmitted. Ordinarily a chemical is released into the space at this
    junction by the first neuron, causing the second neuron to fire. The
    junction between the axon of one neuron and the dendrites of another

    is called a _____.   synapse

32. Transmission at the synapse is only in one direction. You will recall
    that the axons are "senders" and the dendrites "receivers." Therefore,

    the impulse is chemically transmitted across the _____   synapse

    from the _____ of the first neuron to the _____   axon, dendrites
    of the next neuron.

33. Neurons may be classified according to their function. *Afferent* neurons
    carry impulses from the sense organs of the body to the spinal cord and

    brain. Sensory input travels along _____neurons.   afferent

4. *Efferent* neurons carry messages from the brain and spinal cord to the muscles and glands of the body. Messages instigating bodily action are

   carried along _____ neurons.   efferent

35. Acting as middlemen between afferent and efferent fibers are *connecting* neurons. Much of the brain and spinal cord is composed of the nerve

   cells linking sensory and motor nerves that are called _____   connecting
   neurons.

36. Therefore, when a stimulus is received by the sense organs and is transmitted to the brain and a response ensues, the impulses travel from

   _____ to _____ to _____   afferent, connecting,
   neurons.   efferent

37. *Review*
   a. An electrochemical change traveling along a neuron describes a

      nervous _____.   impulse
   b. The "junction" between the axon of one neuron and the dendrites of

      another is the _____.   synapse

   c. Sensory input travels along the _____ neurons.   afferent
      Messages from the brain and spinal cord to muscles and glands

      travel along _____ neurons. The nerve cells that link   efferent

      these sensory and motor nerves are _____   connecting
      neurons.

38. The *central nervous system* is composed of the brain and spinal cord. The spinal cord provides connections for simple reflexes and for the passage of nervous impulses to and from the brain. Together, the brain and

   spinal cord constitute the _____ _____ _____.   central nervous system

39. The brain is diagramed in Figure 8–4. One of two major areas of the brain is the *brain stem*. The lower portion of the brain, connecting with

   the spinal cord, is the _____ _____.   brain stem

40. The first of four major structures within the brain stem is the *medulla*. The medulla helps regulate heartbeat, blood pressure, and breathing.

   Basic processes essential to life are regulated by the _____.   medulla

41. Close to the medulla is the *cerebellum*. The cerebellum controls body balance and coordinates bodily movement. The portion of the brain

   that keeps us right side up is the _____.   cerebellum

42. The *pons* is a group of nerve fibers located in the brain stem and connecting the two sides of the cerebellum and the cerebellum with the

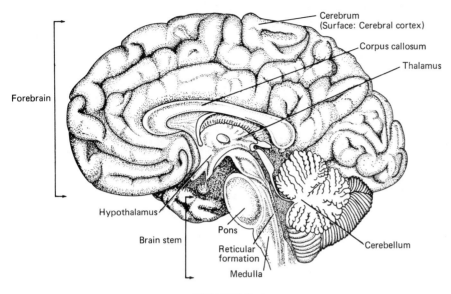

Cerebrum
(Surface: Cerebral cortex)

Corpus callosum

Thalamus

Forebrain

Hypothalamus

Brain stem

Pons

Reticular
formation

Medulla

Cerebellum

FIGURE 8–4

cerebral cortex. The total functioning of the pons is not known, but it appears to be involved in the control of breathing and the rapid eye movements that occur during dreaming. Impulses that cause eye movements when we have nightmares are possibly sent from the _____.

pons

43. The *reticular formation* is a crisscross network of fibers in the brain stem and extending upward. The impulses that the sensory neurons bring to this area stimulate the reticular formation to relay its own impulses to higher centers in the brain. The general state of arousal and activity of these higher brain centers is governed by the impulses

from the _____ _____.

reticular formation

44. *Review*

  a. The brain and the spinal cord compose the _____

     _____ _____.

central

nervous system

  b. The portion of the brain that connects with the spinal cord is the

     _____ _____.

brain stem

  c. Within the brain stem, the center that helps regulate heartbeat, blood

     pressure, and breathing is called the _____.

medulla

  d. The area that coordinates bodily movement and controls balance is

     the _____.

cerebellum

  e. The structure connecting the sides of the cerebellum and possibly involved in the control of breathing and the eye movements dur-

     ing dreaming is the _____, and the structure responsible for the general state of arousal of the higher brain centers is the

pons

     _____ _____.

reticular formation

45. The second major area of the brain is the *forebrain*. The centers for
higher mental processing are located in the _____.   forebrain

46. The *cerebrum* is the large mass covering the top of the brain. The largest
single structure of the brain is the _____.   cerebrum

47. The best-known portion of the cerebrum is its highly convoluted surface, the *cerebral cortex*, which is instrumental in sensory and motor
functions, higher thinking processes, and personality. The area of the
brain that distinguishes man from the lower animals is man's highly developed _____ _____.   cerebral cortex

48. The cerebrum is composed of two *hemispheres*. The left hemisphere
generally controls activity of the right side of the body and the right
hemisphere governs actions of the left side. The two portions of the
cerebrum are called _____.   hemispheres

49. The *corpus callosum* is a nerve bundle located at the base of the cerebrum. Its principal function is to transmit messages between the right
and left hemispheres of the cerebrum. The large nerve bundle that
enables the two hemispheres to cooperate is the _____   corpus
_____.   callosum

50. The way station between the cerebrum and the remainder of the brain
is the *thalamus*. Most messages traveling to and from the cerebrum are
relayed by the _____.   thalamus

51. Another center for connections between higher and lower parts of the
brain is the *hypothalamus*. In addition, the hypothalamus helps regulate
sleep and wakefulness, metabolism, emotional behavior, body temperature, hunger, thirst, and sexual behavior. A center for emotions and
biological needs is the _____.   hypothalamus

52. *Review*

   a. The second major area of the brain is the _____.   forebrain
   b. Within the forebrain is the largest single brain structure, the
   _____, the surface of which, the _____   cerebrum, cerebral
   _____, is divided into two _____.   cortex, hemispheres
   c. The nerve bundle that transfers messages between the right and left
   hemispheres of the brain is the _____ _____.   corpus callosum
   d. A major relay station between the lower and higher structures of the
   brain is the _____.   thalamus
   e. Another connection station, which also plays a role in emotions and
   biological needs, is the _____.   hypothalamus

f. In the diagram below, label each part of the brain and indicate at least one of its functions.

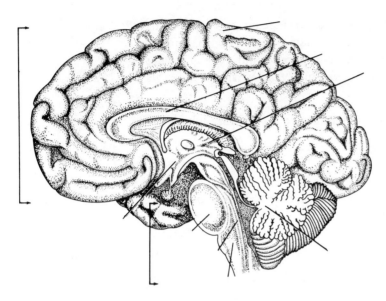

FIGURE 8–5

53. In addition to the central nervous system, there exists the *autonomic nervous system.* Its function is to connect the central nervous system with the heart muscles, the smooth muscles, and the glands of the body. It regulates many bodily activities over which we have little conscious control. For instance, the process of digestion and the rate of heart-

beat are governed by impulses from the _____   autonomic

_____ _____.   nervous system

54. The autonomic nervous system is composed of two parts. One of these is the *sympathetic* division. This portion of the system operates in emergency situations by adjusting heart rate, blood pressure, and breathing, among other things. When your car suddenly skids and you lose control, your quick response is probably being implemented in part by the

_____ division of the _____   sympathetic, autonomic

_____ _____.   nervous system

55. The *parasympathetic* division tends to regulate the same bodily functions as the sympathetic but in times of relative calm rather than emergency. Under ordinary circumstances, pulse, blood pressure, breathing, and digestion,

for example, are managed by the _____   parasympathetic

division of the _____ _____ _____.   autonomic nervous
                                                                           system

56. Both divisions are composed of *ganglia,* which are masses of neuron cell bodies. These cell bodies have dendrites that connect with the central

nervous system and axons that run to the smooth muscles and glands of the body. Clusters of neuron cell bodies in the autonomic nervous

system are known as _____.   ganglia

57. The ganglia of the sympathetic division are arranged in two long chains that parallel the spinal cord, one on either side. In contrast, the ganglia of the parasympathetic division are more scattered about the body, lying near the glands and muscles they affect. Thus, ganglia arranged in rows

near the spinal cord belong to the _____division of   sympathetic
the autonomic system, whereas ganglia that are located throughout the

body belong to the _____ division.   parasympathetic

58. *Review*
    a. The central nervous system receives and processes sensory information; the system that connects the central system with the heart muscles, the smooth muscles, and the glands of the body is the

    _____ _____ _____.   autonomic nervous
                                                                            system
    b. The autonomic nervous system has two divisions. The portion that

    functions in times of emergency is the _____ division,   sympathetic

    while under more ordinary circumstances the _____   parasympathetic
    division would be in control.
    c. Each division is characterized by clusters of cell bodies called

    _____ that either line up along the spinal cord (if they   ganglia

    belong to the _____ division) or are located through-   sympathetic

    out the body (if they belong to the _____   parasympathetic
    division).

self-test

_____ 1. Each human cell except the reproductive cells has
     a. twenty-three chromosomes
     b. forty-six chromosomes
     c. forty-six pairs of genes
     d. twenty-three pairs of genes

_____ 2. The sex of the offspring is determined by the
     a. father's sperm cell
     b. mother's egg cell
     c. mother's blood type
     d. nature of the chemical environ-

ment surrounding the newly fertilized egg

_____ 3. If R is recessive and D is dominant, which pairing is required to produce the trait associated with R?
     a. R-R
     b. R-D
     c. D-D
     d. either R-R, R-D, or D-R

_____ 4. Endocrine glands are
     a. salivation glands

b. ductless glands

c. glands that secrete directly into the stomach

d. glands with ducts

_____ 5. Metabolism determines the amount of

a. hormones in the blood

b. steroids in the blood

c. insulin in the blood

d. energy available in the body

6. At the left are the names of seven endocrine glands. At the right is a list of characteristics and functions. Next to each item in the right-hand column, write the letter of the gland most closely associated with it.

a. pancreas

b. thyroid

c. testes

d. pituitary

e. adrenals

f. ovaries

g. parathyroids

1. located atop the kidneys _____

2. calcium and phosphorus balance _____

3. menstruation _____

4. sudden increase in heart rate _____

5. master gland _____

6. located below the stomach _____

7. activates the sex glands _____

8. cortisol _____

9. blood sugar balance _____

10. normal excitability of nervous system _____

11. underactivity produces sluggishness _____

12. beard _____

13. steroids _____

14. insulin _____

15. dwarfism _____

16. female sex characteristics _____

17. change of voice _____

18. metabolism _____

19. sudden blood sugar increases _____

_____ 7. Axon and dendrite are part of a

a. myelin sheath

b. cell body

c. neuron

d. node

_____ 8. The myelin sheath

a. protects the cell body

b. connects with other neurons

c. groups several neurons together into a nerve fiber

d. facilitates the transmission of a nervous impulse

_____ 9. A functional although not structural connection between neurons is the

a. reticular formation

b. dendrite

c. synapse

d. engram

_____10. Noradrenalin is

a. secreted by the adrenal cortex

b. a depressant

c. important in motor skill

d. found at synapses

_____11. In a typical stimulus-response activity, the sequence in which the neurons fire is

a. afferent, connecting, efferent

b. connecting, afferent, efferent

c. afferent, efferent, connecting

d. efferent, connecting, afferent

_____12. A chemical found to be more abundant in the brains of rats given learning experiences than in those of rats not exposed to these activities is

a. adrenalin

b. cortisol

c. acetylcholine

d. steroid

13. The list on the left names seven parts of the brain; the list on the right contains several functions or characteristics of these parts. Next to each item in the right-hand list, write the letter of the part of the brain most closely associated with it.

a. thalamus
b. hypothalamus
c. medulla
d. cerebellum
e. pons
f. reticular formation
g. corpus callosum

1. body balance _____
2. connects cerebrum with lower brain centers and spinal cord _____
3. involved in control of the emotions _____
4. damage to this structure causes death _____
5. keeps cortex in general state of arousal and activity _____
6. coordinates bodily movement _____
7. connects the sides of the cerebellum _____
8. centers for sleep and wakefulness _____
9. regulates blood pressure _____
10. involved in sexual behavior _____
11. connects two hemispheres of brain _____

_____14. Afferent neurons send side branches to the
a. reticular formation
b. pons
c. cerebellum
d. medulla

_____15. The portion of the brain that contains the hypothalamus and other structures that are involved in emotions and such adaptive behaviors as eating, escaping from danger, and mating is the
a. pons
b. limbic system
c. reticular formation
d. thalamus

_____16. The sensory-motor strip is located along a fissure of the
a. cerebral cortex
b. cerebellum
c. medulla
d. brain stem

_____17. If the rear portion of the cerebral cortex were severely injured, we would expect deficiencies in
a. the sense of pain
b. hearing
c. vision
d. the sense of touch

_____18. The brain waves recorded by an electroencephalograph during quiet wakefulness, when the brain is "at rest," are called
a. beta waves
b. alpha waves
c. expectancy waves
d. electrowaves

_____19. The muscles involved in moving one's legs and arms are called
a. striped
b. smooth
c. cardiac
d. none of the above

_____20. The autonomic nervous system is composed of the
a. cerebrum and motor area
b. cerebral cortex
c. spinal cord and brain
d. sympathetic and parasympathetic divisions

Key to Self-Test

1. (b); 2. (a); 3. (a); 4. (b); 5. (d); 6. (e, g, f, e, d, a, d, e, a, g, b, c, e, a, d, f, c, b, e); 7. (c); 8. (d); 9. (c); 10. (d); 11. (a); 12. (c); 13. (d, a, b, c, f, d, e, b, c, b, g); 14. (a); 15. (b); 16. (a); 17. (c); 18. (b); 19. (a); 20. (d)

exercises

I. The gene producing cataracts is dominant. Suppose that there are only two genes involved in determining this condition, a gene for cataracts (C) and one for noncataracts (NC). If both parents possess a C-NC gene pairing, then the possible pairings in their children are those shown in the table below.

		Mother	
		C	NC
Father	C	C-C	C-NC
	NC	NC-C	NC-NC

There are four possible pairings for the offspring: C-C, C-NC, NC-C, and NC-NC. However, since C is dominant only the child with an NC-NC pairing will not have cataracts. Since it is assumed that any given child is as likely to receive one of the four pairings as another, on the average three out of every four children of this couple will have cataracts. To state it another way, a child of this couple has three out of four chances of having cataracts.

Questions

1. If the father has a C-C and the mother has an NC-NC pairing, what are the possible characteristics of their offspring? What percentage are likely to have cataracts?
2. If your *grandparents* on your father's side had NC-NC and C-NC pairings and your mother possessed the pairing NC-NC, what are the chances that you will have cataracts? What are the chances if your mother possessed the pairing C-NC?
3. If both your father and mother have cataracts, does this mean that you will inevitably have them too? Why or why not?
4. If neither of your parents has cataracts, what are the chances of your having them?

II. In the course of development, several biological changes take place. For example, the child grows bigger and develops secondary sex characteristics. In addition, several vital biological characteristics of the child are constantly kept in a relatively balanced state from moment to moment. For example, muscle tone is maintained and temperature is regulated. The endocrine system plays an important part in these functions of development and daily bodily maintenance. Discuss the regulating role the endocrine system plays in these bodily functions.

III. Consider a man who is asleep on a couch, breathing regularly. Suddenly a sound wakens and alerts him; he sits up and looks around. He stands and has some trouble coordinating himself; he feels cold. Sitting down again, he works a crossword puzzle. Discuss the actions and sensations of this man in terms of what you know about brain functioning. Explain what areas govern which behaviors. Be as specific as possible.

CHAPTER 9 EMOTIONS

programed unit

1. An *emotion* occurs when mental activity is accompanied by *physiological changes*. When we observe such physiological changes as trembling, blushing, and clenched teeth we can assume that the person is experiencing an _____.

    emotion

2. In states of fear and anger, a person's bodily activities are "stirred up." In quieter emotions, such as those of pleasure and relaxation, the body appears to be "toned down." Either way, the emotion is accompanied by _____ _____.

    physiological changes

3. Some of the physiological changes in emotion represent activities of the *striped muscles* of movement, which are normally under *conscious control.* Such physiological changes as muscle tension and tremor represent activities of the _____ _____.

    striped muscles

4. Facial and vocal expressions of emotion also represent activity of striped muscles, which are normally under _____ _____.

    conscious

    control

5. Other physiological changes accompanying emotion are controlled by the *autonomic nervous system* and are not ordinarily under conscious control. When a person's heart begins pounding, his blood pressure rises, and his mouth becomes dry because the salivary glands slow their activity, he is exhibiting physiological changes controlled by the _____ _____ _____.

    autonomic nervous
    system

6. Because heart rate and blood pressure are controlled by the autonomic nervous system, they are not ordinarily under _____ _____.

    conscious

    control

7. *Pupil size,* also controlled by the autonomic nervous system, can be a very sensitive measure of emotion. The wide-eyed look characteristic of rage, excitement, and pain is a result of changes in _____ _____.

pupil

size

8. Pupil size has been found to increase even in such a mild emotion as interest in a photograph. Thus pupil size can be a sensitive measure of _____.

emotion

9. *Review*

a. An emotion occurs when mental activity is accompanied by _____ _____.

physiological changes

b. Physiological changes such as tremor and facial and vocal expressions of emotion represent activity of the _____ _____, which are ordinarily under conscious control.

striped

muscles

c. Other physiological changes accompanying emotion are controlled by the _____ _____ _____.

autonomic nervous
system

d. One physiological change controlled by the autonomic nervous system has been found to be a sensitive measure of even such a mild emotion as interest in a photograph. This is _____ _____.

pupil size

10. The *James-Lange theory* held that the physiological changes sent sensory messages to the brain, and it was these messages that produced the emotion. Thus the James-Lange theory stressed the importance of the _____ changes.

physiological

11. If the physiological changes produce the emotion, then it follows that we do not tremble because we feel afraid but, on the contrary, feel afraid because we are trembling. This was a core idea in the _____-_____ theory.

James-

Lange

12. The *Cannon-Bard theory,* in contrast to the James-Lange theory, stressed *brain activity.* An important theory maintaining that emotion is caused by patterns of brain activity rather than feedback of physiological changes is the _____-_____ theory.

Cannon-Bard

13. According to Cannon-Bard, the *hypothalamus* is the key brain structure in emotion. In this view the hypothalamus is the center of the _____ _____ that produces emotion.

brain activity

14. Cannon-Bard held that the hypothalamus fires off two different kinds of messages: one kind arouses the autonomic nervous system and produces the physiological changes associated with emotion; the other

kind goes to the higher parts of the brain and produces the *feelings* of emotion. Thus the Cannon-Bard theory held that both the physiological changes and the feelings of emotion depend on messages from the

_____.   hypothalamus

15. According to Cannon-Bard, messages from the hypothalamus produce

    not only the physiological changes but also the _____   feelings
    of emotion.

16. Cannon-Bard maintained that both the physiological changes and the feelings of emotion are caused by patterns of brain activity centering

    in the _____.   hypothalamus

17. The newer *cognitive theory* of emotion, based on the work of Schachter, holds that physiological changes are indeed an essential element in emotion and not just a side effect, as Cannon-Bard maintained. In this respect, the cognitive theory is at odds with Cannon-Bard but in partial

    agreement with the _____-_____ theory.   James-Lange

18. According to the cognitive theory, emotions depend on two factors: 1) *physiological changes* and 2) a mental process by which the individual *interprets* or labels his physiological sensations. Thus the idea that an individual may interpret the same kinds of physiological changes in

    different ways is an essential part of the _____ theory.   cognitive

19. The cognitive theory stems from Schachter's experiments—for example, one in which subjects with "stirred up" physiological changes produced by injections of adrenalin acted happy in the company of a happy person and angry in the company of an angry person. In both cases, the subjects presumably experienced the same physiological changes. In one case, they interpreted the changes as the emotion of happiness, in the other as the emotion of anger. Thus the emotion they felt depended on

    how they _____ the physiological changes.   interpreted

20. According to the cognitive theory, the same kinds of physiological changes can be interpreted as different emotions in different environmental contexts. Thus the cognitive theory stresses the importance of

    both 1) _____ changes and 2) the way in   physiological

    which the individual _____ them.   interprets

21. Because of its stress not only on physiological changes but also on the mental process of interpreting the changes, the theory that has grown

    out of Schachter's findings is known as the _____   cognitive
    theory.

22. *Review*
    a. The theory that feedback from physiological changes produces the

       emotion was the _____-_____ theory.   James-Lange

    b. The theory that emotions are caused by patterns of brain activity

       centering in the hypothalamus was the _____-_____   Cannon-Bard
       theory.

    c. A newer theory based on the work of Schachter maintains that
       emotions depend on both 1) physiological changes and 2) a mental
       process by which the individual interprets these changes according

       to what is happening in his environment. This is the _____   cognitive
       theory.

23. Individuals show pronounced *differences* in what kinds of stimuli arouse
    their emotions, the strength of their emotions, and the kinds of behavior
    their emotions produce. Thus emotions, like many other psychological
    phenomena studied since the time of Galton, are subject to a wide range

    of individual _____.   differences

24. Individual differences in emotion are partly the result of *learning*. The
    fact that one person is afraid of snakes and another is not afraid is prob-

    ably due to _____.   learning

25. Differences in emotion may also be caused by differences in activity of
    the *endocrine glands*. The fighting behavior of lions and the fleeing
    behavior of rabbits appear to depend on different kinds of activity of the

    _____ _____ called the adrenals.   endocrine glands

26. People with differences in activity of such endocrine glands as the

    adrenals, pituitary, or thyroid may show wide _____   differences
    in emotion.

27. Individual differences in emotion also appear to be caused by differences
    in the sensitivity of the *autonomic nervous system*. A person with a highly
    sensitive autonomic nervous system may be quicker to display fear or

    anger than a person with a less sensitive _____   autonomic

    _____ _____.   nervous system

28. Emotions are closely related to such *psychosomatic illnesses* as high
    blood pressure and ulcers. Prolonged emtional stress is known to be a

    cause of _____ _____.   psychosomatic illnesses

29. Individual differences in susceptibility to psychosomatic illnesses are

    closely related to individual differences in _____.   emotion

30. *Review*

    a. In the matter of what kinds of stimuli arouse their emotions, the strength of their emotions, and the kinds of behavior their emotions produce, people display a wide range of individual _____.   differences

    b. Since one person may acquire a fear of snakes whereas another does not, individual differences in emotion can be seen to result in part from _____.   learning

    c. Individual differences in emotion also appear to be caused by differences in the activity of the _____ _____   endocrine glands

    and by differences in the sensitivity of the _____   autonomic

    _____ _____.   nervous system

    d. Individual differences in emotion are closely related to individual differences in susceptibility to such _____   psychosomatic

    _____ as high blood pressure and ulcers.   illnesses

31. *Anxiety* is one of the most powerful of emotions and has far-reaching effects on behavior. A vague unpleasant feeling accompanied by a premonition that something undesirable is about to happen is _____.   anxiety

32. Young children are made anxious mostly by possible future events in the external world. To the child, the possibility of punishment or of physical harm from storms and the dark is often a source of _____.   anxiety

33. Adults are most frequently made anxious by feelings of *uncertainty.* When an adult does not know exactly where he stands or what to expect next, he is likely to experience anxiety that stems from feelings of _____.   uncertainty

34. For the adult more often than for the child, feelings of uncertainty are major sources of _____.   anxiety

35. People high in anxiety seem to learn simple tasks more quickly than people low in anxiety but seem to have trouble with more complicated learning. Apparently the intense concentration required for complicated learning is subject to considerable interference from _____.   anxiety

36. Anxiety is also closely related to *risk taking.* People high in anxiety tend either to settle for the "sure thing," and thus avoid failure that would add to their anxiety, or to "go for broke" by taking the kinds of chances at which success is such a remote possibility that failure can be readily excused. Anxiety seems to make them either very conservative or very daring in their _____ _____.   risk taking

37. The kind of risk taking represented by investing a lot of money in a lottery in which there is a very small chance of winning a very large prize would be characteristic of a person _____ in anxiety.   high

38. People who are relatively low in anxiety appear to have sufficient confidence to take the middle-range risks that are most likely to lead to success in the long run. They assume a more successful strategy in risk taking because of their freedom from _____.   anxiety

39. Taking a job that offers a chance for reasonably good pay and that although fairly difficult does not seem hopelessly over his head would be characteristic of a person _____ in anxiety.   low

40. *Review*
   a. A vague unpleasant feeling accompanied by a premonition that something undesirable is about to happen is _____.   anxiety
   b. Anxiety over possible future events in the external world is most common among _____.   children
   c. Adults, on the other hand, are most likely to experience anxiety that stems from feelings of _____.   uncertainty
   d. Anxiety seems to assist in the learning of simple tasks but to hinder more _____ learning.   complicated
   e. Being either very conservative or very daring in risk taking is characteristic of people _____ in anxiety.   high
   f. Assuming the middle-range risks that are most likely to lead to success in the long run is characteristic of people _____ in anxiety.   low

self-test

_____ 1. In emotion, a person's physiological activity is
   a. unchanged
   b. "stirred up"
   c. "toned down"
   d. either "stirred up" or "toned down"

_____ 2. Among the physiological changes in emotion are some that are ordinarily under conscious control because they are activities of the
   a. smooth muscles
   b. autonomic nervous system
   c. striped muscles
   d. hypothalamus

_____ 3. The physiological changes in emotion that are not ordinarily under conscious control are regulated by the
   a. striped muscles
   b. autonomic nervous system
   c. central nervous system
   d. cerebral cortex

_____ 4. The notion that we do not tremble because we are afraid but feel afraid because we tremble is central to the

a. Cannon-Bard theory
b. James-Lange theory
c. cognitive theory
d. all of the above

_____ 5. Secretion of adrenalin is most pronounced in the emotion of
a. fear
b. anger
c. joy
d. grief

_____ 6. Secretion of noradrenalin is most pronounced in the emotion of
a. fear
b. anger
c. joy
d. grief

_____ 7. The Cannon-Bard theory attributes emotion to
a. feedback of sensations caused by physiological changes
b. interpretation by the higher parts of the brain
c. glandular activity
d. patterns of nervous activity fired off by the hypothalamus

_____ 8. In Schachter's experiment, injections of adrenalin
a. had no effect on the subjects
b. made the subjects angry
c. made the subjects fearful
d. had an effect that depended on the subjects' environment

_____ 9. The cognitive theory holds that emotions depend on
a. the mental interpretation of physiological changes
b. feedback from physiological changes
c. patterns of brain activity automatically triggered by the environment
d. mental processes that occur independently of physiological changes

_____10. According to the cognitive theory, the key element in the physiological sensations that accompany emotion is
a. level
b. quality
c. change
d. duration

_____11. When a Chinese schoolboy is scolded, he shows sorrow and shame not by hanging his head but by grinning. This fact demonstrates the role played in emotional behavior by
a. individual differences in the autonomic nervous system
b. inheritance
c. learning
d. conditioning of glandular activity

_____12. Individual differences in capacity for emotion appear to depend on differences in all but which one of the following?
a. striped muscles
b. glandular activity
c. sensitivity of the autonomic nervous system
d. central nervous system

_____13. In Selye's experiments on the effect of stress, the gland that showed the most pronounced changes was the
a. adrenal
b. pituitary
c. thyroid
d. pancreas

_____14. Selye's term for the sequence of events involved in prolonged stress is
a. psychosomatic illness
b. psychological exhaustion
c. general adaptation syndrome
d. emotional disturbance

_____15. Anxiety is most closely related to the emotion of
a. anger
b. grief
c. joy
d. fear

_____16. The bodily states associated with anxiety appear to be closely related to the level in the blood stream of a chemical called
   a. lactate
   b. glycogen
   c. propranolol
   d. insulin

_____17. The chief source of anxiety among adults is
   a. concern over external events
   b. feelings of uncertainty
   c. fear of pain
   d. sexual conflicts

_____18. In the experiment in which subjects were told their chances of receiving a shock, anxiety was highest among those who believed the chances were
   a. 5 percent
   b. 50 percent
   c. 75 percent
   d. 95 percent

_____19. A high level of anxiety is most likely to affect the grades of college students of
   a. low levels of ability
   b. in-between levels of ability
   c. high levels of ability
   d. all the same; no difference

_____20. In risk taking, the person most likely to be very conservative or to "go for broke" is the person whose anxiety level is
   a. low
   b. medium
   c. high
   d. all the same; no difference

Key to Self-Test

1. (d); 2. (c); 3. (b); 4. (b); 5. (a); 6. (b); 7. (d); 8. (d); 9. (a); 10. (c); 11. (c); 12. (a); 13. (a); 14. (c); 15. (d); 16. (a); 17. (b); 18. (a); 19. (b); 20. (c)

exercise

On page 108 is a chart that can be used to list signs of emotion. The next time you have an opportunity to observe your own behavior or that of another person during a state of either 1) anger or 2) fear, anxiety, or embarrassment, put a check mark in the square corresponding to the kinds of behavior you or the other person appears to display. After you have made three observations of yourself and others, the filled-in chart will provide clues to the following questions:

1. Are the external signs of anger (and your own inner feelings) noticeably different from the signs of fear, anxiety, or embarrassment?
2. Do different people display different external signs of the same emotional state?

In all probability, the data from even a few observations will indicate that the answer to question 1 is *no*. As is explained on page 309 of the textbook, feelings of anger are related to secretion of noradrenalin and feelings of fear to secretion of adrenalin; and these two hormones have different effects on certain physiological activities, such as blood pressure. The differences are difficult to observe, however, except with instruments that measure physiological activity.

A few observations will probably also show that different people react in different ways to the same emotional state. The exercise is an illustration of the fact that the bodily changes that take place in emotion—and particularly those that are openly displayed—are not a completely accurate guide to the kinds of emotional feelings that are being experienced.

Signs of emotion	Anger						Fear, anxiety, or embarrassment					
	Self-rating			Other person			Self-rating			Other person		
	1	2	3	1	2	3	1	2	3	1	2	3
1. Blushing or flushed face												
2. Paleness of face												
3. "Wide-eyed" look												
4. Trembling lips												
5. Clenched teeth												
6. Sweaty forehead												
7. Sweaty palms												
8. Trembling hands												
9. Nervous gestures (tapping fingers, tugging at hair, and so on)												
10. Quavery voice												
11. High-pitched voice												
(the following apply only to self-ratings)												
12. "Butterflies in the stomach"												
13. "Hot under the collar"												
14. Fast heart beat												
15. Slow heart beat												
16. Difficulty in breathing												

CHAPTER 10

dRives aNd motives

programed unit

1. Many forms of human behavior are the result of *biological drives,* such as hunger and thirst. Eating and drinking are responses to

   _____ _____.   biological drives

2. Some biological drives occur when the organism is in a state of *deprivation.* The hunger drive occurs because of _____   deprivation

   of food, the thirst drive because of _____ of   deprivation
   water.

3. Deprivation of food triggers the _____ _____   biological drive

   of hunger, deprivation of water the _____   biological

   _____ of thirst.   drive

4. Other biological drives occur when the organism is in a state of *imbalance.* The elimination drive occurs when the organism is in a state of

   _____ because it needs to eliminate its waste prod-   imbalance
   ucts.

5. When the organism needs to sleep or is too hot or too cold, it is also in a

   state of _____ that triggers biological drives.   imbalance

6. Thus either deprivation or imbalance can trigger a _____   biological

   _____.   drive

7. Both deprivation and imbalance are *physiological conditions.* Thus bio-

   logical drives are triggered by certain kinds of _____   physiological

   _____.   conditions

109

8. The physiological conditions that trigger a drive cause patterns of *brain activity*. A biological drive can be defined as a pattern of _____ _____ that results from certain kinds of physiological conditions.

    brain

    activity

9. The pattern of brain activity that constitutes a drive usually results in a *sensation,* such as hunger or thirst. Feeling sleepy is the _____ produced by the pattern of brain activity that constitutes the biological drive for sleep.

    sensation

10. The pattern of brain activity that constitutes a drive also frequently serves as an energizing force that leads to *behavior* designed to end the physiological condition, stop the pattern of brain activity, and thus satisfy the drive. Going to the water fountain is a form of _____ designed to satisfy the thirst drive.

    behavior

11. *Review*

  a. Hunger, thirst, elimination, and sleep are _____ _____.

    biological

    drives

  b. The hunger drive occurs when the organism is in a state of _____ of food; the elimination drive occurs when the organism is in a state of _____ because it needs to eliminate its waste products.

    deprivation

    imbalance

  c. The physiological conditions that trigger a drive cause patterns of _____ _____.

    brain activity

  d. A biological drive, which is a pattern of brain activity brought about by certain kinds of physiological conditions, usually results in a _____, such as hunger or thirst.

    sensation

  e. The pattern of brain activity that constitutes a drive also frequently serves as an energizing force leading to _____ that satisfies the drive.

    behavior

12. In addition to drives, the organism has *stimulus needs;* that is, its basic nature seems to demand some kind of stimulation and especially change in stimulation. The tendencies to seek out new sights to see and new sounds to hear are examples of _____ _____.

    stimulus needs

13. Experiments in which people deprived of all sensory stimulation have experienced inability to remember or think logically indicate that the brain cannot function properly unless the organism satisfies its _____ _____.

    stimulus needs

14. Thus one kind of stimulus need is the need for *sensory stimulation.* In

the experiments in which subjects lost the ability to remember or think logically, they were suffering from lack of _____ _____.

sensory

stimulation

15. Another kind of stimulus need is the need for *stimulus variability*. The tendency to prefer a new recording to one that has been heard many times is an example of the need for _____ _____.

stimulus

variability

16. *Review*
    a. It appears that the brain cannot function properly unless the organism satisfies its basic _____ _____.

    stimulus needs

    b. One kind of stimulus need, satisfied by any kind of stimulation, is the need for _____ _____.

    sensory stimulation

    c. Another kind of stimulus need, satisfied only by a change in stimulation, is the need for _____ _____.

    stimulus variability

17. A *motive* is a desire for a goal that has acquired value for the individual. A desire to help humanity or to become rich and famous is a _____.

motive

18. Unlike drives and stimulus needs, motives appear to depend less on innate factors than on *learning*. The fact that the motive to achieve material success is prominent in some cultures but not in others is an indication that motives are chiefly acquired through _____.

learning

19. One important motive is the motive for *affiliation*. People who show a strong desire for the company and support of others are displaying the motive for _____.

affiliation

20. Behavior stemming from the motive for affiliation is especially common in situations that arouse anxiety. In one experiment, college women made anxious by the possibility of receiving an electric shock preferred to have company rather than to wait alone; these women demonstrated the effect of anxiety on the motive for _____.

affiliation

21. The *achievement motive* is the desire to perform well and to succeed. People who tend to try harder than others and to attain more success in many kinds of situations are likely to rate high in _____ _____.

achievement

motive

22. The *hostility motive* is the desire to see others display signs of worry, fears of discomfort, and actual pain. The argumentative, sarcastic, or

cruel person is displaying the _____ _____.   hostility motive

23. The motive for *certainty* is the desire to understand and predict events and to show consistency between our beliefs and behavior. The desire to know how our friends will behave toward us and what will happen at

    school tomorrow is an example of the motive for _____.   certainty

24. The desire to behave in accordance with our inner standards is also

    an example of the motive for _____.   certainty

25. Closely allied to the motive for certainty, and perhaps a part of it, is what has been called *cognitive consonance,* which means the desire to preserve agreement and harmony among one's thoughts, beliefs, and behavior. When a person whose used car turns out to be a lemon tries to preserve harmony by insisting nonetheless that he got a bargain, he may actually believe what he says because of the desire

    for _____ _____.   cognitive consonance

26. Humanistic psychologists accept Maslow's theory that human beings have a motive for *self-actualization,* an innate inclination to seek beauty, goodness, truth, and the fullest possible development of their own unique potentialities for perfection and creativity. An artist who is willing to starve in a garret while seeking to perfect his skills is exhibiting what humanistic psychologists would call the motive for

    _____-_____.   self-actualization

27. *Review*
    a. A desire for a goal that has acquired value for the individual is a

       _____.   motive

    b. Motives appear to depend less on innate factors than on _____.   learning
    c. The desire for the company and support of others is the motive for

       _____.   affiliation

    d. The desire to perform well and to succeed is the motive for

       _____.   achievement

    e. The desire to see others suffer discomfort is the _____   hostility
       motive.
    f. The desire to understand and predict events is the motive for

       _____.   certainty

    g. Closely allied to or part of the motive for certainty is the desire to preserve agreement and harmony among one's thoughts, beliefs, and behavior, which is the desire for _____   cognitive

       _____.   consonance

    h. Humanistic psychologists accept the theory that human beings have an innate desire for beauty, goodness, truth, and development of their own potentialities, called the motive for _____- self-

_____. actualization

28. *Motivational dispositions* are the sum total of all the motives a person has acquired. They are not always in active awareness or operation. When a person has a desire to visit Europe someday but does not ordinarily

think about it, we call this desire a _____ motivational

_____. disposition

29. A motivational disposition is a *potential* influence on one's thinking and behavior. A motivational disposition to go to Europe someday, which is

not now in active awareness, is a _____ influence on potential
the person who holds it.

30. An *aroused motive* is one that an individual is thinking about at any given moment. If the motivational disposition to go to Europe comes into active awareness when one looks at a travel advertisement, it becomes an

_____ _____. aroused motive

31. Whereas a motivational disposition is only a potential influence on one's

thinking and behavior, an _____ _____ is an aroused motive
active influence.

32. *Freud* introduced the idea that people have *unconscious motives,* that is, wishes and desires that they are never aware of but that influence their behavior nonetheless. A man who honestly denies that he has any motives for hostility yet can be observed to perform many subtle acts of aggression toward his family and associates is behaving in accordance with

what Freud would call _____ _____. unconscious motives

33. The importance of unconscious motives was first stressed by _____. Freud

34. *Functional autonomy* is the principle that an activity that is originally a means to an end frequently acquires an independent function of its own and becomes an end or motive in itself. A businessman who starts out by working hard to satisfy his motives for achievement and security and then continues to work hard long after he is wealthy illustrates the

principle of _____ _____. functional autonomy

35. *Review*
    a. The sum total of all the motives a person has acquired are his

_____ _____. motivational
dispositions

    b. A motivational disposition is only a _____   potential
       influence on one's thinking and behavior.

    c. A motive that the individual is thinking about at any given moment is

       an _____ _____.   aroused motive

    d. An aroused motive is an _____ influence on one's thinking   active
       and behavior.

    e. Freud introduced the idea that behavior can be influenced by

       _____ _____.   unconscious motives

    f. The principle that an activity that is originally a means to an end
       frequently acquires an independent function of its own and becomes

       an end or motive in itself is called _____   functional

       _____.   autonomy

36. A motive leads to goal-related behavior only when certain requirements are met. Thus a motive may not have any effect at all on

    _____.   behavior

37. One requirement that must be met if a motive is to lead to behavior
is *knowledge of how to satisfy the motive.* The adolescent who has a
strong motive for the companionship of the other sex yet does not
know how to be attractive probably will not undertake any goal-

    related behavior because of lack of _____ of how   knowledge

    to _____ the motive.   satisfy

38. In addition to having knowledge of how to satisfy the motive, we must
also have an *incentive.* The motive must be triggered into behavior
by something that arouses it. A bulletin board notice of tryouts for a
college play might arouse the motive for achievement in drama by

    serving as an _____.   incentive

39. *Expectation of success* is also necessary if a motive is to produce behavior. Even if a student considers the tryout notice an incentive, he
will probably take no action unless he thinks he has a chance to get

    into the cast and therefore a reasonable _____   expectation

    ____ _____.   of success

40. *Freedom from anxiety* is another requirement for behavior. If the student
interested in the tryout notice is afraid to appear in public, he may

    refrain from action because he is not free from _____.   anxiety

41. *Absence of conflicting motives* is the final requirement for behavior. The
student may not go to the tryout if he also has a strong motive to study at
the same hour or watch a favorite television show. He is likely to behave

in accordance with his motive to go to the tryout only in the absence of

_____ _____.   conflicting motives

42. *Review*
  a. Unless certain requirements are met, a motive may have no effect

     at all on _____.   behavior
  b. A person who does not know how to be attractive to the opposite
     sex may not behave in accordance with his motive for sexual com-

     panionship because of lack of _____ of how to   knowledge

     _____ the motive.   satisfy
  c. A motive must be triggered into behavior by an _____   incentive
     that arouses it.
  d. A person who believes he has no chance of satisfying his motive may

     refrain from goal-related behavior because he lacks _____   expectation

     ____ _____.   of success

  e. Goal-related behavior also depends on freedom from _____.   anxiety

  f. Behavior is also likely to take place only in the absence of _____   conflicting

     _____.   motives

self-test

_____ 1. A pattern of brain activity that results
       from certain kinds of physiological
       conditions is a(n)
       a. motive
       b. stimulus need
       c. drive
       d. incentive

_____ 2. The center for feelings of hunger is
       the
       a. stomach
       b. throat
       c. mouth
       d. brain

_____ 3. The proportion of time spent in
       paradoxical sleep as opposed to
       ordinary sleep is
       a. 10 percent
       b. 20 percent

       c. 50 percent
       d. 80 percent

_____ 4. Rapid eye movements are characteris-
       tic of
       a. daydreaming
       b. reading
       c. ordinary sleep
       d. paradoxical sleep

_____ 5. Drives are triggered by events in the
       environment called
       a. stimuli
       b. goals
       c. consummatory actions
       d. incentive objects

_____ 6. The need for sensory stimulation
       appears to be
       a. inborn

b. acquired in the second month of life
c. acquired at about age one
d. learned at various stages of development

_____ 7. A person who pays to hear a new jukebox record or watch lights flash on a pinball machine is chiefly satisfying his
a. biological drives
b. need for sensory stimulation
c. need for stimulus variability
d. motives

_____ 8. "Pacer stimuli" are most closely related to
a. sensory stimulation
b. stimulus variability
c. sensory thresholds
d. ideal level of complexity

_____ 9. Motives appear to depend mostly on
a. drives
b. stimulus needs
c. learning
d. inborn tendencies

_____ 10. Behavior stemming from the affiliation motive is most likely to occur
a. among men rather than women
b. in situations that arouse anxiety
c. among those who were not first-born in the family
d. among those high in hostility

_____ 11. An automobile driver who gets into trouble either for going too slow or for reckless driving is likely to be low in the motive for
a. affiliation
b. achievement
c. certainty
d. hostility

_____ 12. Living up to standards is most closely connected with the motive for
a. affiliation
b. achievement

c. certainty
d. hostility

_____ 13. The desire for cognitive consonance is most closely connected with the motive for
a. affiliation
b. achievement
c. certainty
d. hostility

_____ 14. What kind of influence are motivational dispositions on thinking and behavior?
a. potential
b. active
c. unconscious
d. negligible

_____ 15. Freud contributed to our knowledge of what kind of motives?
a. potential
b. active
c. unconscious
d. autonomous

_____ 16. A businessman who starts out by working hard for achievement and security but continues to work hard long after he is successful and wealthy demonstrates the principle of
a. unconscious motives
b. functional autonomy
c. persistence of motivational dispositions
d. aroused motives

_____ 17. A motive leads to goal-related behavior
a. in all cases
b. when motivational dispositions are strong
c. when a motivational disposition becomes an aroused motive
d. only when certain conditions are met

_____ 18. The external event that triggers a motive into behavior is a(n)

a. arousal
b. expectation of success
c. incentive
d. consummatory action

_____19. A student with a strong motive for achievement has an opportunity to spend his evening studying for a good grade or trying out for a college drama; he chooses the tryout. We can assume that success in the drama has greater
a. strength of arousal
b. functional autonomy
c. unconscious appeal
d. incentive value

_____20. An emotion that frequently prevents motives from resulting in behavior is
a. anxiety
b. complacency
c. hostility
d. euphoria

Key to Self-Test

1. (c); 2. (d); 3. (b); 4. (d); 5. (d); 6. (a); 7. (c); 8. (d); 9. (c); 10. (b); 11. (b); 12. (c); 13. (c); 14. (a); 15. (c); 16. (b); 17. (d); 18. (c); 19. (d); 20. (a)

exercises

I. On the chart at the right, keep a record for a week of when you go to bed and when you get up, noting also the total number of hours you have slept. (Even if you have trouble falling asleep or awaken before it is time to get up, count all the time from going to bed to getting up as hours spent in sleep.) Also keep a record on the chart of how you felt in general the next day. Get some friends to keep the same kinds of records.

Your own chart, when completed, may offer some useful indications of how much sleep you require to feel your best the next day. And a comparison of your chart with the charts of your friends may show some rather striking individual differences. As is explained in the textbook (page 337), some people prefer to go to bed late and rise late, others to go to bed early and get up early. Moreover, some people feel perfectly fine if they get as little as five or six hours of sleep, whereas others require as much as nine or ten hours to feel their best.

If you have access to a fever thermometer, it is also useful to keep track of your temperature during the week at several times of the day: 1) immediately on arising, 2) at noon, 3) at 5 P.M., and 4) just before going to bed. Record your temperature on the chart on page 118. In general,

Sleep during week

	S	M	T	W	T	F	S
Went to bed							
Got up							
Total hours of sleep							

Physical and mental state next day

Felt unusually good and alert						
Slightly above par						
Average						
Slightly below par						
Sleepy, not able to concentrate						

you are likely to feel best and be most efficient at times of the day when your temperature is highest (usually around 98.6 degrees). You are likely to feel sleepy and inefficient when your temperature is below this level. Temperature is another respect in which rather wide individual differences exist. Some people show a temperature of around 98.6 degrees early in the morning, others not until later in the day. Those whose temperature is relatively high early in the day usually show a drop by evening; those whose temperature does not reach its peak until later often are still near the peak even at bedtime. The thermometer will provide an objective measure of whether you are a "day person" or a "night person." The practical value of knowing which you are is that "day people" function better when they can arrange to do their work or studying as early in the day as possible, whereas "night people" function best if they can arrange their chores to fall late in the day and in the evening.

Temperature during week

	S	M	T	W	T	F	S
Arising							
12 noon							
5 P.M.							
Before bed							

II. As is explained in the text on page 348, first-born children and only children have generally been found to rank higher in achievement motive than children who have older brothers and sisters. To conduct your own survey, pick out from among your acquaintances as many as possible who seem to have a strong motive for achievement—for example, acquaintances who seem to strive very hard for success in their studies, athletics, or other activities. Be careful, however, not to confuse striving for success with success itself. Some people are very successful in their studies or in athletics simply because they have a great deal of ability, not because they work particularly hard at seeking success. Conversely, some people who are very high in achievement motive attain only modest success because they lack ability.

Once you have selected a list of acquaintances who seem to be obviously high in achievement motive, find out how many of them are the only child in the family, how many are first-borns, and how many are later-born children. Your survey will of course not be as objective as a scientist would like, because you will have to depend on your own judgment of strength of achievement motive. Nor will your sample probably be large enough to ensure reliable results. Nonetheless, you may find some rather striking relationships between achievement motive and position in the family. The results will be especially interesting if you arrange to compare the people high in achievement motive with an informal "control group" of other acquaintances who seem to be low in achievement motive.

CHAPTER 11

frustration, conflict, and abnormal behavior

programed unit

1. One meaning of *frustration,* referring to external events, is the blocking of motive satisfaction by an *obstacle.* If the motive to be in class on time is blocked by the obstacle of a traffic jam, the traffic jam creates

   _____.   frustration

2. The traffic jam represents an example of frustration created by the

   blocking of motive satisfaction by an external _____.   obstacle

3. Another meaning of frustration, referring to internal sensations, is the *unpleasant feelings* that result from the blocking of motive satisfaction by

   an obstacle. In the internal sense, frustration means _____   unpleasant

   _____.   feelings

4. The unpleasant feelings called frustration result from the blocking of

   _____ satisfaction.   motive

5. Individuals display rather wide differences in the kinds of external events they find frustrating. Thus an obstacle may be considered as a

   _____ by one person but not by another.   frustration

6. Individuals also differ widely in the intensity of the unpleasant feelings of frustration caused by the blocking of motive satisfaction. The

   same obstacle may cause more of the _____   unpleasant

   _____ of frustration in one person than in another.   feelings

7. *Review*
   a. Referring to external events, frustration is the blocking of motive

   satisfaction by an _____.   obstacle

119

     b. Referring to internal sensations, frustration is the _____   unpleasant

     _____ that result from the blocking of motive satis-   feelings
     faction.

     c. People display rather wide individual differences in the kinds of

     external _____ they consider to be frustrating.   obstacles

     d. People also display individual differences in the intensity of the

     _____ _____ called frustration.   unpleasant feelings

8. A *conflict* is created by the simultaneous arousal of two or more incompatible motives. When we simultaneously desire to study and to

    go to a movie, we experience a _____.   conflict

9. An essential part of the definition of conflict is that it results in *unpleasant emotions,* including anxiety. When one is torn between studying
and going to a movie, he is in conflict because of the simultaneous arous-

    al of incompatible motives, which results in _____   unpleasant

    _____.   emotions

10. One type of conflict occurs between *motives* and *internal standards.*
When a student is tempted to cheat on an examination to get a good
grade but feels inwardly that cheating is wrong, he is experiencing a con-

    flict between a motive and an _____ _____.   internal standard

11. In our society, women often experience conflict between the motive
to be independent and dominant and the belief that women should
display dependent and submissive behavior. This represents a conflict

    between a motive and an _____ _____.   internal standard

12. Men often are torn between the urge to be dependent and the masculine
standard calling for independent and even aggressive behavior. This,

    too, is a conflict between a _____ and an _____   motive, internal

    _____.   standard

13. Another type of conflict occurs because of the arousal of two motives
aimed at different and incompatible *external goals.* When a person is
torn between studying and going to the movies, he is in conflict because

    his motives are aimed at two incompatible _____   external

    _____.   goals

14. Two motives aimed at external goals that frequently conflict are
achievement and *affiliation.* A student who wants to make a good
grade but does not want to lose the friendship of his classmates by
doing better than they do is experiencing a conflict between the motives

    for _____ and _____.   achievement, affiliation

15. An *approach-approach* conflict occurs when the aroused motives are directed toward two desirable goals, both of which a person wants to approach. When a student wants to stay up and watch the late-night movie on TV but simultaneously wants to get a good night's sleep, he is in an _____-_____ conflict.

approach-approach

16. An *avoidance-avoidance* conflict occurs because of the simultaneous arousal of motives to avoid two alternatives that are both *un*pleasant. A student, too keyed up to sleep, wants to avoid the unpleasantness of tossing and turning in bed, yet also wants to avoid the grogginess he will feel the next day if he takes a sleeping pill. The student is in an _____-_____ conflict.

avoidance-avoidance

17. An *approach-avoidance* conflict occurs when a person has mixed emotions about a goal that has both desirable features (making him want to approach it) and undesirable features (making him want to avoid it). A student who wants to follow the school team to an out-of-town game but dislikes the idea of traveling so far is in an _____-_____ conflict.

approach-
avoidance

18. *Review*
   a. The simultaneous arousal of two or more incompatible motives, resulting in unpleasant emotions, is a _____.

conflict

   b. An essential part of the definition of conflict is that it results in _____ _____, including anxiety.

unpleasant emotions

   c. One type of conflict occurs between motives and _____ _____.

internal
standards

   d. Another type of conflict results from the simultaneous arousal of two motives aimed at different and incompatible _____ _____.

external
goals

   e. When the conflict is between motives directed toward two desirable goals, this is an _____-_____ conflict.

approach-approach

   f. When the conflict is between motives to avoid two alternatives that are both *un*pleasant, this is an _____-_____ conflict.

avoidance-
avoidance

   g. When a person has mixed emotions about a goal that has both desirable and undesirable features, this is an _____-_____ conflict.

approach-
avoidance

19. The unpleasant emotions caused by conflict and frustration often result in important forms of behavior. One is *aggression*. When a

child, frustrated by another child who takes his toy, strikes out with his fists, he is attempting to relieve his unpleasant feelings through

_____.   aggression

20. Some people react to frustration and conflict by displaying *depression,* including the extreme form known as apathy. When a person lives his days in a hopeless "blue funk" because he feels helpless to cope with his frustrations and conflicts, he is displaying the extreme form of

_____ called apathy.   depression

21. Others tend to display *withdrawal;* they try to avoid any kind of goal-seeking activity that might result in further frustrations, conflicts, and anxiety. When a person "retreats into a shell," avoids social contacts, and instead lives in a fantasy world of daydreams of love and success, he is

displaying _____.   withdrawal

22. Another frequent result of conflict is *vacillation,* in which a person is drawn first toward one resolution of the conflict, then toward another. A student spending so much time trying to decide whether to study or go out with his friends that he finally has no time for either is a good

example of _____.   vacillation

23. In *regression,* especially common among children, the individual retreats toward types of behavior appropriate to a lower level of maturity. A frustrated child who goes back to such forgotten habits as thumb sucking and wanting to be fed from a bottle is displaying

_____.   regression

24. Another reaction to frustration and conflict is *stereotyped behavior,* in which a person tends to repeat some action over and over again, even though it appears to serve no useful purpose. A person who constantly tends to repeat certain phrases, whether or not they are appropriate to

the conversation, may be displaying _____   stereotyped
behavior.

25. Besides having effects on behavior, frustration and conflict may result in mental processes called *defense mechanisms,* which represent *unconscious* attempts to reduce anxiety. Unconscious attempts to relieve

the anxiety caused by frustration and conflict are _____   defense
mechanisms.

26. Although there are many forms of defense mechanisms, all of them

represent _____ attempts to relieve anxiety.   unconscious

27. Perhaps the most common of all defense mechanisms is *rationalization,* which represents an attempt to relieve anxiety by deciding that one has

not really been frustrated or that a conflict has not occurred. Aesop's fable about the fox, unable to reach the grapes, that consoled itself by deciding they would have been sour anyway is a good example of

_____.   rationalization

28. *Review*

   a. Striking out at the cause of frustration, as when a child uses his fists

   or an adult kicks a flat tire, is _____.   aggression

   b. Reacting to frustration and conflict by feeling blue and unable to

   cope with one's problems is _____.   depression

   c. Avoiding social contacts and goal-seeking activities that might result

   in further frustrations, conflicts, and anxiety is _____. withdrawal

   d. Being drawn first toward one resolution of a conflict, then toward

   another, is _____.   vacillation

   e. When a frustrated child goes back to such forgotten habits as thumb

   sucking, he is displaying _____.   regression

   f. When a person suffering frustration or conflict shows a tendency to

   repeat some action over and over again, he is displaying _____ stereotyped
   behavior.

   g. Mental processes that represent unconscious attempts to reduce the

   anxiety caused by frustration and conflict are called _____   defense
   mechanisms.

   h. A student who, after failing to make the team, convinces himself that he did not want to waste his time on athletics anyway is probably adopting the common defense mechanism known as

   _____.   rationalization

29. Reactions to frustration and conflict form one important aspect of the difference between the *normal personality* and the *abnormal personality*. The person who can function more or less successfully despite frustrations, conflicts, and the anxiety they produce is displaying a

   _____ personality.   normal

30. The person who cannot function at all is an extreme example of an

   _____ personality.   abnormal

31. One characteristic of abnormal behavior is that it is *statistically unusual*. Since only a few Americans believe in witches, a belief in witches is likely to be taken as an indication of abnormality because it is statistically

   _____.   unusual

32. Another characteristic of abnormal behavior is that it is considered *strange* or *undesirable* by most people in the society. A man who walks

down the street talking loudly to himself is considered abnormal partly

because his behavior seems _____ and _____.   strange, undesirable

33. A third characteristic of abnormal behavior is that it is a source of *unhappiness* to the person who displays it. The person who is miserable because of an ungovernable temper is considered abnormal partly be-

cause his behavior causes him _____.   unhappiness

34. Abnormal behavior is closely related to *stress*. "Battle fatigue," the breakdown sometimes experienced by soldiers who have coped success- fully with many difficult problems in civilian life, is an example of

abnormal behavior caused by _____ beyond the individual's   stress
capacity for endurance.

35. Individual differences in ability to tolerate stress appear to depend in part on *biological factors*. Tolerance for stress is affected by inherited differences in glandular activity and sensitivity of the nervous system,

both of which are _____ factors.   biological

36. Differences in biological factors account in part for the differences in the

ability to _____ stress.   tolerate

37. Individual differences in ability to tolerate stress also depend on *psy- chological factors*. The person who has acquired extremely high internal standards that are difficult to live up to is especially likely to suffer stress

because of _____ factors.   psychological

38. A third group of factors influencing tolerance for stress are *cultural factors* (or social factors). The fact that the severe form of mental dis- turbance called schizophrenia is most common among people born in

the slum areas of big cities indicates the importance of _____   cultural
or social factors.

39. *Review*
   a. The person who functions more or less successfully despite frustrations,

      conflicts, and the anxiety they produce displays a _____   normal
      personality.
   b. The person who cannot function at all is an extreme example of

      an _____ personality.   abnormal
   c. Abnormal behavior is defined as behavior that is statistically

      _____, considered by most people in the society to be   unusual

      strange or _____, and a source of _____   undesirable,
      to the person who displays it.   unhappiness

d. The breakdown known as "battle fatigue" demonstrates the fact that abnormal behavior is closely related to _____.   stress

e. Individual differences in ability to tolerate stress depend on inherited _____ factors such as glandular activity and   biological

sensitivity of the nervous system, on _____   psychological
factors such as the internal standards a person has acquired, and on

social or _____ factors.   cultural

40. A *psychoneurosis,* usually shortened to *neurosis* in popular usage, is a twilight zone form of abnormality lying between normal behavior and the extreme form of disturbance called psychosis. A person whose behavior is not normal but who is not so disturbed as to be called psychotic

is suffering from a _____.   psychoneurosis

41. Although there are many forms of psychoneurosis, all are characterized by high levels of *anxiety,* displayed in various types of behavior. The

characteristic common to all psychoneuroses is a high level of _____.   anxiety

42. A *psychosis* is a form of mental disturbance that is so severe as to make a person incapable of getting along in society. The condition known in popular terminology and legal language as insanity is referred to by psychologists and psychiatrists as _____.   psychosis

43. An *organic psychosis* is one clearly caused by a physiological condition. An elderly person who becomes unable to function in society because of brain damage due to hemorrhages of blood vessels is suffering from

an _____ psychosis.   organic

44. A *functional psychosis* is one that has no clear-cut physiological explanation. When no medical test as yet available shows anything wrong with the brain, but the brain simply does not seem to be working properly,

the patient is said to be suffering from a _____   functional
psychosis.

45. The most common functional psychosis is *schizophrenia,* in which the most striking characteristic is extreme disturbance of thought indicated by such symptoms as illogical speech, the invention of new and bizarre words and ideas, and sometimes hallucinations (imaginary sensations) and delusions (false beliefs). A patient who imagines that bugs are crawling under his skin or believes that he is already dead is probably

suffering from _____.   schizophrenia

46. *Manic-depressive psychosis* is characterized by extremes of mood. A patient who is wildly active and restless or so gloomy and hopeless that

he refuses to eat, or who swings between these two extremes of mood,

is probably suffering from _____-_____   manic-depressive
psychosis.

47. *Paranoia* is a rare form of functional psychosis characterized by delusions of grandeur or of persecution. A patient who believes that he is
Napoleon ruling the world or that everybody is trying to kill him is

probably suffering from _____.   paranoia

48. An abnormality different from either psychosis or psychoneurosis is
psychopathic personality (also called sociopathic personality). The
psychopath (or sociopath) seems to lack a conscience or sense of social
responsibility and to have no feeling for other people. The criminal
who seems to experience no remorse for even the most cruel kinds of

deeds is an extreme example of _____   psychopathic
personality.

49. *Review*
  a. A twilight zone form of abnormality lying between normal behavior

  and extreme disturbance is a _____.   psychoneurosis
  b. The characteristic common to all psychoneuroses is a high level of

  _____.   anxiety
  c. A mental disturbance so severe as to make a person incapable of

  getting along in society is a _____.   psychosis
  d. A psychosis that is clearly caused by a physiological condition is

  an _____ psychosis.   organic
  e. A psychosis that has no clear-cut physiological explanation is a

  _____ psychosis.   functional
  f. The most common functional psychosis, characterized by extreme

  disturbances of thought, is _____.   schizophrenia
  g. Extremes of mood — wildly active or hopelessly gloomy — are charac-

  teristic of _____-_____ psychosis.   manic-depressive
  h. A rare form of psychosis characterized by delusions of grandeur or

  persecution is _____.   paranoia
  i. Lack of conscience, sense of social responsibility, and feeling for
  other people is characteristic of the abnormality known as socio-

  pathic or _____ personality.   psychopathic

self-test

_____ 1. A man who is perfectly satisfied with his salary until his best friend gets a raise, and then feels unhappy, illustrates
   a. frustration by a physical obstacle
   b. frustration by a personal obstacle
   c. frustration by a social obstacle
   d. the relative nature of frustration

_____ 2. Tolerance of frustration
   a. cannot be changed by special training
   b. is displayed more by children than by adults
   c. is subject to wide individual differences
   d. characterizes people of high intelligence

_____ 3. To be classed as a conflict, the simultaneous arousal of two or more incompatible motives must result in
   a. vacillation
   b. a situation to which there is no solution
   c. defense mechanisms
   d. unpleasant emotions

_____ 4. A child who wants to strike out angrily against his parents but at the same time wants to be an obedient child who respects his parents illustrates
   a. a conflict between a motive and an internal standard
   b. a conflict over external goals
   c. vacillation
   d. frustration

_____ 5. In our society, the motive to avoid success is most likely to result in conflicts for
   a. children
   b. women
   c. college men
   d. adolescents

_____ 6. The kind of conflict experienced by a student who simultaneously wants to watch a late movie on television and to get a good night's sleep is best described as
   a. approach-avoidance
   b. double approach-avoidance
   c. approach-approach
   d. avoidance-avoidance

_____ 7. The gradient of approach is
   a. at its lowest level near the goal
   b. about as steep as the gradient of avoidance
   c. steeper than the gradient of avoidance
   d. influenced by the strength of the motive involved

_____ 8. Scapegoating is a good example of
   a. direct aggression
   b. displaced aggression
   c. stereotyped behavior
   d. a defense mechanism

_____ 9. A person who avoids goal-seeking behavior and instead lives in a make-believe world of daydreams is reacting to frustration or conflict with
   a. withdrawal
   b. depression
   c. vacillation
   d. regression

_____10. The first-born child who reacts to the birth of another child in the family by resuming such old habits as thumb sucking and wanting to be fed from a bottle is displaying
   a. withdrawal
   b. depression
   c. vacillation
   d. regression

_____11. Defense mechanisms are *not*
   a. mental processes

b. attempts to relieve anxiety
c. a form of self-deception
d. conscious

_____12. The behavior of Aesop's fox, deciding that the grapes it could not reach would have been sour anyway, represents a literary description of the defense mechanism called
a. rationalization
b. projection
c. repression
d. reaction formation

_____13. A person, anxious over his own strong tendencies toward dishonesty, accuses everyone else of being dishonest. He is displaying the defense mechanism called
a. rationalization
b. projection
c. repression
d. reaction formation

_____14. The normal personality is all but which one of the following?
a. free of conflicts and anxiety
b. realistic
c. spontaneous
d. tolerant of other people's limitations

_____15. Abnormal behavior is all but which one of the following?
a. defined similarly in all societies
b. statistically unusual
c. considered strange or undesirable by most people
d. a source of unhappiness

_____16. Whether a person will or will not develop the symptoms of abnormal behavior depends chiefly on
a. the kinds of frustrations he encounters

b. the kinds of conflicts he experiences
c. individual differences in use of defense mechanisms
d. individual differences in tolerance for stress

_____17. A phobic reaction is one form of
a. obsessive-compulsive reaction
b. hysteria
c. anxiety state
d. psychosis

_____18. A person who becomes unable to get along in society in his old age is probably suffering from
a. a functional psychosis
b. an organic psychosis
c. schizophrenia
d. manic-depressive psychosis

_____19. A person who has delusions of grandeur or persecution is likely to be suffering from
a. schizophrenia
b. psychopathic personality
c. paranoia
d. manic-depressive psychosis

_____20. A criminal who shows no remorse for a brutal crime is most likely showing the symptoms of
a. schizophrenia
b. psychopathic personality
c. paranoia
d. manic-depressive psychosis

Key to Self-Test

1. (d);   2. (c);   3. (d);   4. (a);   5. (b);   6. (c);
7. (d);   8. (b);   9. (a);   10. (d);   11. (d);   12.
(a);   13. (b);   14. (a);   15. (a);   16. (d);   17.
(c);   18. (b);   19. (c);   20. (b)

exercise

Following is a case history that raises some interesting problems related to normal and abnormal behavior.

John L.

Now sixty-three, John L. recently took early retirement from the production department of a large book publisher in New York City, a job he had held for forty-one years. He and his wife now live comfortably in a small apartment in Florida on a company pension and Social Security.

At the publishing house, John L.'s work record was perfect except for one incident in which he got into a fist fight with a fellow worker whom he accused of refusing to pay a football bet. The other man claimed that John L. had cheated him on the bet by claiming that the point spread was higher than it actually was. Others in the department reported that this was not unusual—that in fact John L. frequently tried to win bets in this fashion and that most of them had quit betting with him.

When he retired, John L. told the company physician that he had become physically unable to put in the long hours that his job often required. His wife, however, believes that he had become afraid to ride the New York subways, particularly after working late. Her belief is shared by some of his fellow workers, who noticed that his conversation had become increasingly concerned with the muggings and burglaries reported in the New York newspapers.

John L. was formerly a fan of horse and dog racing, at which he was a small but consistent winner, but he now goes to the tracks infrequently. When he does go, he carries only small amounts of money and invariably tries to park his car in the most crowded and well-lighted part of the lot.

If he wins any considerable sum, he leaves the track immediately, as if afraid he might be followed and robbed. He does not trust banks and keeps his money spread among three of them in small accounts. His wife is concerned because he has never made a will, on the grounds that lawyers are crooked and charge too much for their services.

John L. is apparently happy in his retirement, though he leads a life that most people would consider rather quiet and restricted. His wife complains that they seldom go out except to a movie—always a matinee, in broad daylight. They do not eat at restaurants because John L. believes that restaurant food is dirty and overpriced. Indeed their chief activity, aside from reading and watching television, is an annual trip to visit a married son in a small town in Michigan. John L. often says that he would like to move to this town, where people are more honest than in the cities, but that he dislikes the northern winters.

Questions

1. Do any of the defense mechanisms seem apparent in John L.'s behavior? If so, which ones?
2. Being excessively afraid of being robbed or cheated by a bank or lawyer is the kind of behavior often popularly described as "paranoid." Does John L.'s behavior suggest the possibility of the psychosis called paranoia?
3. Where on a scale from normal behavior through psychoneurosis through psychosis would John L. seem to fall?
4. If he were a relative, would you be inclined to recommend psychotherapy?

CHAPTER 12
PERSONALITY THEORY AND PSYCHOTHERAPY

programed unit

1. *Personality* is defined in part as a person's ways of thinking, feeling, and behaving. Such traits as thinking logically or illogically, feeling cheerful or sad, and behaving in a friendly or unfriendly manner are all parts of

   the human _____.   personality

2. To be considered a personality trait, a way of thinking, feeling, and behaving must be *characteristic* of the individual. We do not call a man bad-tempered if he "blows up" only once in ten years. But if he displays a bad temper often and under many circumstances, it is a personality

   trait because it is _____ of him.   characteristic

3. Personality traits are also *distinctive;* that is, they distinguish the individual from other individuals. Since many people carry a driver's license,

   doing this is not a personality trait because it is not _____.   distinctive

4. In addition, personality traits constitute the individual's method of *relating to his environment.* Although wearing a ring may be characteristic and distinctive, it is not a personality trait because it plays no significant

   part in _____ to one's environment.   relating

5. Being friendly and outgoing is a personality trait because it does play a

   significant part in _____ to one's environment.   relating

6. Personality is defined as the *total pattern* of characteristic ways of thinking, feeling, and behaving that constitute the individual's distinctive method of relating to his environment. Thus personality is not just a

   single trait, such as a bad temper, but the individual's total _____   pattern
   of traits.

130

7. *Review*

   a. A person's ways of thinking, feeling, and behaving go to make up

      his _____.   personality

   b. To be considered a part of personality, a trait must be displayed often and under many different kinds of circumstances—that is, it

      must be _____ of the person.   characteristic

   c. The trait must distinguish the individual from other individuals—that

      is, it must be _____.   distinctive

   d. The trait must also constitute a method of _____ to   relating
the environment.

   e. Thus personality is defined as the total _____ of   pattern
characteristic ways of thinking, feeling, and behaving that constitute an individual's distinctive method of relating to his environment.

8. One theory of the origins and dynamics of personality is the *psychoanalytic theory,* developed by Freud. The important personality theory

   originated by Freud is the _____   psychoanalytic
theory.

9. Freud was a pioneer in emphasizing the role of *anxiety,* which he believed to be the central problem in mental disturbance. Thus psychoanalytic theory stresses the importance of the troublesome emotion

   called _____.   anxiety

10. Freud also originated the concept of the *unconscious,* composed partly of repressed motives and thoughts. A man who is not aware of hostile motives but displays them in ways observable by others demonstrates

   the workings of the _____.   unconscious

11. According to psychoanalytic theory, the mind has three parts. One, which is the core of the unconscious, is the *id,* composed of raw, primitive, inborn forces that constantly struggle for gratification. To Freud, the primitive and compelling drives toward sex and aggression consti-

   tute a part of the mind that he called the _____.   id

12. The individual is not aware of the powerful demands of the id; therefore

   the id is an _____ part of the mind.   unconscious

13. Freud called the conscious, logical part of the mind the *ego.* The conscious and sensible part of the mind—what might be termed the "real"

   us, as we like to think of ourselves—is the _____.   ego

14. To the extent that the primitive drives of the id can be satisfied without danger or damage, the ego permits them satisfaction. But when the

unconscious demands of the id threaten to get the individual jailed or rejected by society, they are suppressed in various ways by the conscious _____.   ego

15. The third part of the mind is the *superego,* a largely unconscious but stern and powerful judge of behavior that threatens to punish the ego relentlessly for any transgression or even thought of transgression. Thus the ego is in a constant struggle to satisfy the primitive drives of the id without incurring the wrath and vengeance of the _____.   superego

16. To Freud, a person who is a selfish and hot-headed menace to society represents a failure of the ego to check the primitive drives of the _____.   id

17. A person who suffers vague and unwarranted feelings of unworthiness, and sometimes an unconscious need for self-punishment, represents a case in which the ego is overwhelmed by that largely unconscious but powerful judge of behavior called the _____.   superego

18. *Review*
    a. Freud developed the _____ theory   psychoanalytic
       of personality.
    b. Among the ideas advanced by Freud was the importance of the troublesome emotion called _____.   anxiety
    c. Freud also originated the concept that many important aspects of the mind are not in awareness but instead are _____.   unconscious
    d. Of the three parts of the mind as conceived by Freud, the core of the unconscious, composed of raw, primitive drives toward sex and aggression, is the _____.   id
    e. The conscious, logical part of the mind is the _____.   ego
    f. The largely unconscious part of the mind that operates as a stern judge of behavior is the _____.   superego

19. *Social learning theories,* in contrast to psychoanalytic theory, regard personality as habitual ways of responding to the environment, learned in accordance with the standard principles of learning. Personality theories that emphasize the role of learned habits in personality are _____ _____ theories.   social learning

20. Social learning theories hold that behavior reinforced by *reward,* particularly from other members of society, tends to become habitual. Thus a child praised by his parents for independent behavior might become an independent adult because he has received _____   reward
    for that kind of behavior.

21. On the other hand, behavior that meets with *punishment* tends to be abandoned. A child severely and constantly chastised for speaking his

    mind might grow into a meek adult because _____   punishment
    has molded his behavior patterns.

22. Social learning theories also emphasize the role of *observation learning.*

    A child might become a strong, reliable adult through _____   observation
    and imitation of strong, reliable parents.

23. *Review*
    a. Theories that regard personality as learned, habitual ways of re-

       sponding to the environment are _____   social learning
       theories.
    b. To understand a person's personality and predict his behavior, according to the social learning theorists, we would have to know which of his actions have been reinforced in the past through

       _____, which have been discouraged by _____,   reward, punishment
       and also what kinds of people and actions he has come to imitate

       through _____ learning.   observation

24. *Psychotherapy,* based on personality theories, is the treatment of personality disorders through psychological methods. A person who seeks help for a personality difficulty by talking to a psychologist or psychiatrist or participating in an encounter group is trying to solve his prob-

    lems through _____.   psychotherapy

25. *Psychoanalysis* is the form of psychotherapy associated with the psychoanalytic theory of personality. Followers of Freud practice the form

    of therapy known as _____.   psychoanalysis

26. The goal of psychoanalysis is to give the patient *insight* into the unconscious processes of his mind and his unconscious conflicts, so that he can deal with and control these processes. According to psychoanalysis, the patient can only solve his problems by gaining control over his

    unconscious processes through _____.   insight

27. To help the patient acquire insight, psychoanalysts use the tool of *free association.* The patient who is encouraged to lie relaxed on a couch and speak out every thought that occurs to him is using the psychoanaly-

    tic tool of _____.   free association

28. The psychoanalyst listens carefully for signs that the patient is encountering *resistance,* that is, when his thoughts seem to be blocked by anxiety and repressions indicating unconscious conflict. One way to give

the patient insight into his unconscious processes is to analyze the

blocks to free association caused by _____.   resistance

29. Another phenomenon analyzed by the psychoanalyst is *transference,* which is the tendency of the patient to transfer to the people he now knows the emotional attitudes he had as a child to such much-loved and much-hated persons as his parents, brothers, and sisters. If the patient behaves as if the analyst were a much-admired but much-feared father, the analyst assumes that this is a case of the tendency

    called _____.   transference

30. By analyzing the patient's free associations, resistances, and transferences, the psychoanalyst attempts to help the patient acquire insight

    into his _____ mental processes and conflicts.   unconscious

31. *Review*
    a. The treatment of personality disorders through psychological methods is _____.   psychotherapy
    b. The form of psychotherapy associated with the psychoanalytic theory of personality is _____.   psychoanalysis
    c. The goal of psychoanalysis is to give the patient _____ into his unconscious mental processes and conflicts.   insight
    d. In asking the patient to lie relaxed on a couch and blurt out all his thoughts, the analyst is using the tool of _____ _____.   free association
    e. The psychoanalyst carefully looks for blocks in the patient's thinking, called _____, and for any tendency of the patient to transfer childhood emotional attitudes to the analyst or other people, called _____.   resistance   transference
    f. By analyzing the patient's free associations, resistances, and transferences, the psychoanalyst attempts to help the patient toward insight into his _____ mental processes and conflicts.   unconscious

32. *Behavior therapy* is a method of psychotherapy that has grown out of social learning theories. A therapist who regards the symptoms of the patient (or client) as learned habits that can be changed through re-

    learning is practicing _____ therapy.   behavior

33. One method used by behavior therapists is *extinction,* an attempt to eliminate a conditioned response that is causing the patient trouble. For example, a behavior therapist who treats stuttering as a conditioned response that can be eliminated in various ways, just as the salivary

response of Pavlov's dog disappeared when the reinforcement of food was withdrawn, is using the method of _____.   extinction

34. Behavior therapists also use *reinforcement* to establish new habits that will be more successful than the old. When patients in a mental hospital are rewarded for improvement in behavior with movie or TV privileges, their therapist is using the method of _____.   reinforcement

35. *Desensitization* is a method used by behavior therapists to treat phobias by associating the stimulus that has caused the fear with relaxation rather than with fearful behavior. A therapist who treats a fear of elevators by helping his client stay relaxed while thinking about elevators is practicing _____.   desensitization

36. Behavior therapists also use *observation learning* to help their clients acquire more successful kinds of behavior. Treatment of a snake phobia by having the client watch other people handle snakes without fear is an example of the method of _____ learning.   observation

37. *Group therapy* is the simultaneous treatment of several clients at a time, rather than in an individual meeting between the therapist and a single patient. The currently popular encounter groups and sensitivity groups are both forms of _____ therapy.   group

38. Group therapy has been used by many therapists of various schools of thought, including some psychoanalysts. The fact that there are not enough therapists available to treat all prospective patients individually is one reason for the growth of _____ therapy.   group

39. *Review*
   a. The form of therapy that has grown out of social learning theories is _____ therapy.   behavior
   b. When a behavior therapist tries to eliminate a symptom by treating it as a conditioned response that can be made to disappear much as the salivary response of Pavlov's dog eventually disappeared, he is using the method of _____.   extinction
   c. When a behavior therapist rewards forms of behavior that will be more successful than old habits, he is using the method called _____.   reinforcement
   d. Eliminating phobias by associating the stimulus that has caused fear with relaxation is called _____.   desensitization
   e. When a behavior therapist asks a client to watch and imitate more successful behavior, he is using the method of _____ learning.   observation

f. Treatment of several clients at a time, rather than individually, is

_____ therapy.   group

40. Totally different from psychotherapy is *medical therapy,* in which
physicians, usually psychiatrists, attempt to treat personality disorders
through medical means. A psychiatrist who gives a patient medicine
designed to relieve his personality problems by changing the chemical

processes in the brain is practicing _____ therapy.   medical

41. One important form of medical therapy is *chemotherapy,* so named
because it relies on the use of medicines (which are chemical com-
pounds). Thus the psychiatrist who prescribes a medicine for a disturbed patient is practicing the particular form of medical therapy

known as _____.   chemotherapy

42. Among the most widely used medicines in chemotherapy are the *tranquilizers,* which slow down the excessive nervous activity in the brain that is
characteristic of anxiety, hallucinations, and delusions. Because schizophrenic patients display extreme anxiety and sometimes hallucinations

and delusions, they are often treated with _____.   tranquilizers

43. Also important in chemotherapy are the *psychic energizers,* which speed
up nervous activity in the brain. Since patients suffering from depression appear to have reduced brain activity, they can often be treated suc-

cessfully with the _____ _____.   psychic energizers

44. Another form of medical therapy is *electroshock therapy,* in which elec-
tricity is passed through the patient's brain. Like the psychic energizers,
electroshock therapy appears to produce an increase in brain activity.
Therefore patients suffering from depression can be treated either with

the psychic energizers or with _____ therapy.   electroshock

45. *Review*
   a. Treatment of personality problems through medical means is

   _____ therapy.   medical
   b. The particular form of medical therapy that relies on medicines

   (which are chemicals) is _____.   chemotherapy
   c. Prominent among the medicines used in chemotherapy are a group

   that reduce brain activity; these are called _____.   tranquilizers
   d. Other medicines speed up nervous activity in the brain; these are

   called _____ _____.   psychic energizers
   e. A form of medical therapy used to treat depression by passing an

   electric current through the patient's brain is _____   electroshock
   therapy.

self-test

_____ 1. The emotion considered by Freud to be the central factor in personality disturbance is
a. anxiety
b. anger
c. love
d. hate

_____ 2. According to Freud, the core of the unconscious is the
a. id
b. ego
c. superego
d. none of the above

_____ 3. According to Freud, the part of the mind that operates on the reality principle is the
a. id
b. ego
c. superego
d. none of the above

_____ 4. What Freud called the Oedipus complex is most closely related to the
a. id
b. ego
c. superego
d. pleasure principle

_____ 5. Which one of the following men considered the libido a life force that includes deep-seated attitudes toward life and death, virtue and sin, and religion?
a. Freud
b. Jung
c. Adler
d. Hartmann

_____ 6. The term "inferiority complex" was first used by
a. Freud
b. Jung
c. Adler
d. Hartmann

_____ 7. The importance of the ego was stressed by
a. Freud
b. Jung
c. Adler
d. Hartmann

_____ 8. Social learning theories of personality emphasize
a. reflex behavior
b. operant behavior
c. unconscious motives
d. rewards and punishments

_____ 9. Self theories of personality are most closely connected with the name of
a. Fromm
b. Rogers
c. Bandura
d. Miller

_____10. The type of therapy developed by Rogers is
a. transference
b. behavior therapy
c. desensitization
d. client-centered therapy

_____11. Behavior therapy is an outgrowth of
a. social learning theories
b. psychoanalytic theory
c. neo-psychoanalysis
d. self theories

_____12. The baby cured of vomiting through use of electric shocks is an example of
a. electroshock therapy
b. extinction
c. reinforcement
d. desensitization

_____13. The token economy used in some mental hospitals is a form of the behavior therapy technique called
a. extinction
b. reinforcement

c. desensitization

d. observation

_____14. The experiment on the elimination of snake phobia indicated the importance of the behavior therapy technique called
   a. extinction
   b. reinforcement
   c. desensitization
   d. observation

_____15. Family therapy is a form of
   a. interactional therapy
   b. chemotherapy
   c. client-centered therapy
   d. free association

_____16. Which one of the following statements is *not* true of group therapy?
   a. It has been used by some psychoanalysts.
   b. It is in part the child of necessity.
   c. It has no genuine advantages over individual therapy.
   d. It may relieve anxiety.

_____17. Which one of the following is *not* characteristic of the most successful psychotherapists?
   a. They like their patients.
   b. They have empathy toward their patients.
   c. They are themselves suffering from strong anxieties.

   d. They have treated many previous patients.

_____18. People who do not receive psychotherapy will recover from their neuroses
   a. never
   b. occasionally
   c. perhaps in as many as 40 percent of cases
   d. perhaps in as many as 75 percent of cases

_____19. Tranquilizers appear to be effective for some disturbed people because they
   a. reduce the sensitivity of synapses in the brain
   b. act directly on the sympathetic nervous system
   c. increase the level of brain activity
   d. stop excessive glandular activity

_____20. Chemotherapy does *not* utilize
   a. tranquilizers
   b. psychic energizers
   c. electroshock
   d. amphetamines

Key to Self-Test

1. (a); 2. (a); 3. (b); 4. (c); 5. (b); 6. (c); 7. (d); 8. (d); 9. (b); 10. (d); 11. (a); 12. (b); 13. (b); 14. (d); 15. (a); 16. (c); 17. (c); 18. (d); 19. (a); 20. (c)

exercise

The self theory of personality proposed by Carl Rogers, as explained on pages 412–14 of the textbook, centers around the concept of the *phenomenal self*—that is, the image of himself that each person perceives in his own unique fashion. This image may or may not correspond to reality or to what the person would like to be. Indeed some rather striking differences along these lines have been found between "normal" people and those with personality problems. The normal person tends to show a fairly close correspondence between his image of himself and the way he would like to be, or his ideal image, indicating that he is reasonably satisfied with the phenomenal self that he perceives. The person with personality problems tends to show little or no similarity between what he thinks he is and what he would like to be, indicating that he is quite dissatisfied with his phenomenal self.

With the help of the items on page 141, you can perform an informal experiment that will give you at least a rough idea of the relationship between what you think you are and what you would like to be. The experiment is based on the study described on pages 412–13 of the textbook.* To perform it, cut out the sixteen items into the rectangles indicated by the lines. Shuffle them, put them on a desk or table in random order, and then arrange them in a line going from your left to your right. At the extreme left, place the statement that you think describes you best. At the extreme right, place the statement that you think is most untrue about you. In between, arrange the remaining cards in the order ranging from most true to least true. When you have finished, use the table on page 140 to write down the order of the cards as you have arranged them, from 1 at the extreme left to 16 at the extreme right; do this under "Rank on list 1."

Next reshuffle the cards, place them in front of you again, and this time arrange them in an order that best describes not what you are but what you would like to be. Put the statement that you wish were most true of you at the extreme left, the one you wish were least true of you at the extreme right. When you have completed this pattern of what you would like to be, again use the table on page 140 to write down the order of the cards as you have arranged them, this time under "Rank on list 2."

For a rough measure of how your phenomenal self differs from your ideal self, note the difference in the rank of each card from list 1 to list 2, disregarding whether it ranked higher on list 1 or list 2. For example, if card A was 6 on list 1 and 8 on list 2, the difference is 2; if card A was 8 on list 1 and 6 on list 2, the difference is also 2. Total the differences. The smaller the total, the greater is the correspondence between what you think you are and what you would like to be. The average person usually shows a total difference of between about 50 and 60. A difference as low as 35 shows a rather rare correspondence between phenomenal self and ideal self; a score of more than 75 indicates a rather low correspondence. However, if you score 75 or even much higher, do not leap to the conclusion that you are suffering from a personality problem. On a short and informal test such as this, many factors can influence the result. The exercise is designed only to cast some light on the Rogers theory, not to diagnose personality.

By doing a little further arithmetic, you can get a more accurate measure. For each card, square the number found in the column showing difference in rank, and enter the square in the column called "Difference squared." Then total the numbers you have just placed in this column. Divide the total by 680, and subtract the answer from 1.

What you have just done is compute a coefficient of correlation, which is a statistical measure of the relationship between two factors, by the rank-difference method described on pages 461–62 of the textbook (one indication that psychological statistics are not so difficult as students often assume). In the Butler and Haigh study, the average correlation between phenomenal self and ideal self for subjects who had never sought therapy was .58; for subjects who were being treated for personality problems it was zero. However, the Butler and Haigh study and the informal experiment in this exercise differ in important ways, and the results are not completely comparable. Moreover, it must again be pointed out that the experiment is not intended as a diagnosis of personality, and a zero or even a minus correlation is not to be considered alarming.

*Butler, J. M., and Haigh, G. V. Changes in the relation between self-concepts and ideal concepts consequent upon client-centered counseling. In Rogers, C. R., and Dymond, R. F., eds. *Psychotherapy and personality change: coordinated studies in the client-centered approach.* Chicago: University of Chicago Press, 1954, pp. 55–76.

Card	Rank on list 1	Rank on list 2	Difference in rank	Difference squared
A				
B				
C				
D				
E				
F				
G				
H				
I				
J				
K				
L				
M				
N				
O				
P				
Total of differences				
Total of squared differences				

$$\text{Correlation coefficient} = 1 - \frac{(\text{Total of squared differences})}{680} = \underline{\qquad}$$

I usually manage to stay even tempered. A	I consider myself a leader. I
I spend too much **time** daydreaming. B	I am a shy person. J
I am a very likable person. C	I am physically attractive. K
I have to admit that I am rather selfish. D	I often feel blue and discouraged. L
I can work as hard as anybody when I want to. E	I am more intelligent than most people. M
I have a hard time standing up for myself. F	I worry about what other people think of me. N
Nothing frightens me. G	I have a good sense of humor. O
I often feel tense around other people. H	I wouldn't be above cheating. P

CHAPTER 13

MEASUREMENT

programed unit

1. *Measurement* is the assignment of numbers to traits, events, or objects according to some kind of orderly system. Therefore, determining the number of responses an organism makes by counting them is a form

   of _____.   measurement

2. The *statistical method* is the application of mathematical principles to the interpretation of numbers. The careful analysis of psychological data in order to arrive at appropriate conclusions frequently utilizes the

   _____ _____.   statistical method

3. The statistical method is based on the laws of *probability*. The probability of an event is the likelihood that it will occur in a given situation. For example, on the average we expect a coin to come up heads one time in two; this fact is expressed in a ratio, $\frac{1}{2} = .50$, which is the

   _____ of a head turning up in a single toss of   probability
   a coin.

4. Probability gives us the percentage of such situations in which a specific event will occur. In the situation of rolling a die, on the average we would expect one-sixth or 16.7 percent of the rolls to turn up a six.

   Therefore, .167 is the _____ of a six in a roll of   probability
   a die.

5. Frequently, our intuitive conception of probability differs from the actual probability value. For example, when a person gets a bridge hand composed of all thirteen spades, he considers it a fantastically improbable event. It is, but every other hand of thirteen specific cards is equally

   improbable; the _____ of *any* particular bridge   probability
   hand is about 1 in 159 billion.

6. *Review*

    a. A psychological researcher attempts to assign numbers to his observations according to the orderly process of _____.   measurement

    b. These measurements are then analyzed and interpreted through the application of certain mathematical principles, that is, according to the _____ _____.   statistical method

    c. A statement about the likelihood that the results would occur as they did is made according to the laws of _____.   probability

7. The form that the orderly assignment of numbers in measurement takes is called a *scale*. Inches, pounds, temperature, rank in class, and categories of automobiles are examples of _____ of measurement.   scales

8. Scales differ from one another on the basis of whether they possess one or both of two general properties. The first property is an absolute *zero*. An absolute zero is the point at which no amount of the quality being measured exists. For the scale of length in inches, 0 inches is the absolute _____.   zero

9. The second property is *equal intervals*. If a scale has equal intervals there is an equal amount of the quality being measured between each unit on the scale. Thus, the difference between the values of 1 and 2 is the same as between 101 and 102 or between 45 and 46 if the scale has _____ _____.   equal intervals

10. A scale is called a *ratio* scale when it possesses both a zero point and equal intervals. Weight in pounds, length in inches, and time in seconds are all _____ scales.   ratio

11. Specifically, 0 pounds means no weight at all, indicating the presence of an absolute zero. Further, the difference between 6 and 7 pounds equals that between 78 and 79 pounds, demonstrating the property of equal intervals. Therefore, the scale of weight in pounds possesses both an absolute _____ and _____ _____.   zero, equal intervals

    Weight in pounds is an example of a _____ scale.   ratio

12. We call weight in pounds a ratio scale because ratio statements may be made. For example, if a father weighs 200 pounds and his son weighs 100 pounds, the father is twice as heavy as his son. Such statements can only be made about _____ scales.   ratio

13. Not all scales contain both the general properties of absolute zero and equal intervals. For example, an *interval* scale possesses equal intervals

but not an absolute zero point. Temperature in degrees is an example

of an ———————— scale.   interval

14. Although the difference between 10 and 20 degrees is the same as between 70 and 80 degrees, it is not true that 60 degrees is twice as hot as
30 degrees. This is because the temperature scale as we customarily
measure it has equal intervals but not an absolute zero, and therefore

it is an ———————— scale.   interval

15. An *ordinal* scale has neither a zero point nor equal intervals. It is a scale
on which individuals are arranged in order of rank. Academic rank in

class is an example of an ———————— scale.   ordinal

16. An ordinal scale possesses only the property of relative magnitude; that
is, one measure is either more than, equal to, or less than another. If
people in the class are ranked according to their height, the heights of
those ranked 1 and 2 may differ by several inches while the difference
between the heights of those ranked 10 and 11 may be only a fraction
of an inch. The ranking scale calls these intervals equal ($2 - 1 = 1$;
$11 - 10 = 1$), although in terms of height they are not. Therefore,

ranking constitutes an ———————— scale.   ordinal

17. The *nominal* scale lacks even the crude relative magnitude represented
by ranking. In the nominal scale, numbers designate different categories.
Makes of automobiles or positions on a football team that are cate-

gorized into groups constitute a ———————— scale.   nominal

18. *Review*
a. The application of numbers to traits according to an orderly system

produces a ——————— of measurement. Scales can be character-   scale

ized on the basis of whether they possess an absolute ———————   zero

point and ——————— ————————————.   equal intervals
b. A scale having both these properties and permitting relative compari-

sons is called a ——————— scale. If a scale possesses equal inter-   ratio

vals but not a zero point it is an ———————— scale.   interval
c. If the numbers are ranked and reflect only relative magnitude it is

an ———————— scale, and if a scale merely classifies things   ordinal

into groups it is a ———————— scale.   nominal
d. For example, temperature in degrees is an ————————   interval

scale, time in seconds is a ——————— scale, designation of styles   ratio

of furniture by category is a ————————scale, and the ranking   nominal

of the top ten basketball teams in the country is an _____   ordinal
scale.

19. Galton found that many of the traits he measured formed a distribution
that when plotted made a bell-shaped curve, known as the *normal curve*
of distribution. Most traits or events tend to cluster about the average,
with the number declining as either the lower or the upper extreme
values are approached. When plotted on a graph, these traits or events

form a bell-shaped curve, called a _____ _____ of   normal curve
distribution.

20. For example, if you were to consider the heights of thirteen-year-old
boys, most cases would fall near the average height, with progressively
fewer cases representing the very short or tall boys. Many traits, such as

height, weight, and I.Q., form a _____ _____ of   normal curve
distribution.

21. Much of the statistical method is based on this curve. Since so many
traits follow its general pattern and since we know much about the
mathematical properties of this curve of distribution, statisticians use
it as a standard against which to evaluate their results. Their statistical

basis is the _____ _____ of distribution.   normal curve

22. If you wanted to describe how well your class did on an examination,
it would be inconvenient to list every score. One function of *descriptive
statistics* is to provide a quick and convenient method of summarizing
the nature of any group of measures. The characterization of a group

of measurements can be accomplished by using _____   descriptive

_____.   statistics

23. One of the easiest quantities to determine in descriptive statistics is the
number of subjects or cases, a quantity called *N*. Obviously we would
think differently about the fairness of a coin if it came up heads on
twenty consecutive tosses rather than on just two. Therefore, the num-

ber of cases, symbolized by ___, is an important characteristic of one's N
observations.

24. A very common descriptive measure is the average value of a group of
scores. The sum of all the score values divided by the number of cases
defines the arithmetic average, which is called the *mean*. The mean
represents one measure of central tendency. In a normal curve of dis-

tribution most scores tend to have a value near the _____.   mean

25. Another measure of central tendency is the *median*. The median is the
score value that divides the group of scores into two halves. That is,
50 percent of the scores in a group fall above and 50 percent fall below

the _____.   median

26. In a perfectly symmetrical normal curve of distribution the mean and the median are the same value. However, in curves that are not symmetrical the median may be a more representative measure of central tendency than is the mean. For example, in the group

1, 2, 3, 4, 100

the *mean* is 22, but this does not reflect the group trend as well as does the *median,* which is 3. In this case the most representative statistic is

the ——————— rather than the ————.   median, mean

27. A last measure of central tendency is the *mode.* The mode is simply the most frequent score. If a group of scores consists of

1, 2, 2, 3, 3, 3, 4, 5

the value of 3 would represent the ————.   mode

28. Sometimes a group of scores will look like this:

1, 2, 3, 4, 5, 5, 5

Although the mean is 3.6 and the median is 4, it is helpful for descrip-

tive purposes also to know that 5 is the ————.   mode

29. *Review*
    a. When a plot of a group of scores forms a bell-shaped pattern, the

       distribution is said to follow the ——————— ————— of   normal curve
       distribution.
    b. One of the purposes of statistics is to summarize characteristics of
       a group of measures. The fulfillment of this purpose is the task of

       ——————————— ———————————.   descriptive statistics
    c. One number that describes the measures is the number of subjects

       or cases, symbolized by ——. N
    d. Further, in order to describe a group of scores we must determine
       the average value. There are three measures of central tendency: the

       arithmetic average, called the ————; the score value that   mean

       divides the group into two equal parts, or the ———————;   median

       and the most frequent score, or the ————.   mode

30. However, knowing the average of a group of scores does not fully characterize the group. For example, consider these two groups of scores:

A: 5, 7, 9
B: 1, 7, 13

Both groups A and B have the same mean and median, but they differ in the *variability* of the scores. Variability refers to the extent to which the scores differ from one another. Clearly, the scores in group B have

more ——————————— than those in group A.   variability

31. The easiest way to describe the variability in a group of scores is to give the *range*. A crude way to determine the range is to subtract the lowest score from the highest. For group A the _____ is 4, while for group B the range is ____.

range

12

32. A more sophisticated description of variability than the range is the *standard deviation,* abbreviated SD. The standard deviation is a numerical value, computed from the scores of the group, that reflects the extent to which the scores deviate from one another. A more accurate measure of variability than the range is the _____

_____, or ____.

standard

deviation, SD

33. A large standard deviation indicates large variability. The standard deviation of 5, 7, 9 is 2, while the SD of 3, 7, 11 is 4. The more variability, or the greater the deviation of the scores from one another, the greater the _____ _____.

standard deviation

34. Although the measures discussed above can describe a group of scores very well, they do not help us to characterize an individual score. Suppose you received an 85 on your psychology exam. The score alone lacks meaning unless it can be compared to the scores of your classmates. If you were told that a score of 85 was at the 75th *percentile,* you would know much more about your performance. A percentile indicates the proportion of cases that fall below a given score. If three-quarters of the people in your class scored below you, you would be at approximately the 75th _____.

percentile

35. *Review*
    a. One characteristic of a group of scores is how much the individual scores differ from one another, that is, the _____ of the scores.

variability

b. A simple measure of variability is obtained by subtracting the lowest score in the group from the highest. The result is called the _____. A more sophisticated index of variability is the _____ _____.

range

standard deviation

c. The position of an individual score in a group is described by its _____.

percentile

36. Besides description, another aspect of statistics is called *inferential statistics.* Inferential statistics are procedures that permit generalizations to be made from measurements. When a psychologist performs an experiment on a group of male students at his university, he may wish to generalize the results to all male college students by using _____ _____.

inferential statistics

37. Usually there is a large group of subjects to which the researcher would like to generalize his conclusions. This larger group of subjects is called the *population* (or universe). In the above example, all college males constitute the group receiving the generalization and are therefore the

    _____.   population

38. However, it is impractical to use every member of the population in the experiment. Usually a *sample* is selected. A sample is a small group of subjects drawn from the population. Twenty-five males at State Uni-

    versity might be a _____ from the larger _____   sample, population
    of all college males.

39. In order to permit generalizations the sample must be *representative*. That is, the sample must reflect all aspects of the population in their appropriate amounts. In public opinion polling, for example, members of all ethnic, religious, and income groups must be selected in ap-

    propriate numbers for the sample to be _____.   representative

40. An important aspect of a representative sample is that it ordinarily must be chosen at *random*. That is, each member of the population must have an equal opportunity to be included in the sample. If a pollster interviews the occupant of every fifth house in a town, he has

    selected a _____ sample of home dwellers.   random

41. *Review*
    a. Procedures that permit generalizations to be made from measure-

       ments are called _____ _____.   inferential statistics

    b. In research, usually a smaller group, or _____, is drawn   sample

       from the larger _____.   population
    c. If this sample faithfully reflects all aspects of the population, it is

       said to be _____.   representative
    d. If each subject in the population had an equal opportunity to be

       selected, the sample is a _____ sample. Generalizations   random

       can then be made to the larger _____ on the   population

       basis of the results obtained from the _____.   sample

42. Suppose a researcher wants to know if administering a certain drug to rats facilitates learning a simple problem. He selects two random and representative samples of rats and gives the drug to one group and a neutral substance to the other. He finds that the drugged group had a mean of 41 correct responses and the nondrugged group a mean of 35 correct responses on the test problem. The researcher would like to know if this difference was due to *chance*. That is, even if both groups were treated precisely alike, one would not expect them to have the

same average score. In this case the difference between the two groups

could have been a _____ difference.   chance

43. Earlier in this unit the concept of *probability* was discussed. The probability of an event is the likelihood or percentage of times a given event
will occur. Therefore, the researcher might ask what the probability is
that the difference he observed between the two groups was merely a
function of chance factors and not of the drug. That is, what is the

_____ that the result is due to _____   probability, chance
and not to the drug?

44. If the probability is very small that the result is due to chance, the difference is statistically *significant*. If in the example above the probability
is small that the difference between the means is due to chance, the
groups probably differ because of the influence of the drug. The dif-

ference is then statistically _____.   significant

45. The term *significant* implies "nonchance." Therefore, a difference that is

probably *not* a function of _____ factors is _____.   chance, significant

46. How small does the probability that the observed difference is due to
chance have to be in order to decide the difference is significant, that is,
not due to chance? Customarily, psychologists demand that the probability that the difference is due to chance be .05 (5 chances in 100) or
less for the difference to be called significant. Thus, if the likelihood,

or _____, that an observed difference would   probability

be found by random or _____ factors is only 5 times or less   chance

out of 100, the difference is termed statistically _____.   significant

47. *Review*
    a. The likelihood that a given event will occur is its _____.   probability
    b. If the likelihood that an observed difference would be found by

        _____ factors is only 5 times or less out of 100, the difference chance

    is considered statistically _____.   significant

48. The significance of the difference between the means of two groups is
not the only information researchers might desire. They also might
want to know the *correlation,* or relationship, between two different
measures. If two measurements—for example, I.Q. and college grades—

are related, it is said that a _____ exists between   correlation
them.

49. The degree of correlation between two measures is reflected in a numerical index called the *correlation coefficient.* The degree to which two

measures are related is expressed by the _____   correlation

_____ .   coefficient

50. The correlation coefficient has a value of $+1$ if the two measures have a perfect *positive* relationship. For example, if you work for $2.50 an hour, the relationship between hours worked and wages will be perfect and both measures will increase together. The correlation coefficient

would be $+1$ because there is a perfect _____ cor-   positive
relation between hours worked and wages.

51. But two measures can have a *negative* rather than a positive correlation. In professional football, the team that finishes last in the league during the season is given first choice of the graduating college players for the next year. This inverse relationship between league standing and

sequence of selecting new players is a perfect _____   negative
correlation, written -1.

52. Sometimes there is no relationship at all between two measures. The correlation coefficient is then equal to 0. For example, there is no relationship between I.Q. and ability at pitch discrimination. Therefore, the

value of this _____ _____   correlation coefficient

is __.   0

53. Most pairs of measures are not perfectly related. Rather, they have correlations somewhere between -1 and $+1$. For example, the correlation between I.Q. and college grades is approximately .50. This implies that there is a moderately positive relationship between the two measures. That is, there is a moderate tendency for students with high I.Q.'s to get high college grades. A correlation coefficient may range

between ____ and ____. If no relationship exists, it equals __. $-1, +1, 0$

54. Just because two measures are related does not mean that one *causes* the other. Because the sun comes out shortly after a milkman wakes up in the morning does not mean that his rising causes the sun to shine. Therefore, a correlation between two measures implies that values on one measure are related to values on another, but this does not mean

that one _____ the other.   causes

55. *Review*

a. If two measures are related, a _____ exists   correlation
between them. If high values on one measure are associated with high

values on the other, a _____ correlation exists. If   positive
high values on one are associated with low values on another, a

_____ correlation exists.   negative

b. A numerical index of the degree of relatedness is known as the

_____ _____.   correlation coefficient

c. The value of the correlation coefficient ranges between ____ and   — 1

____; if no relationship at all exists, its value is __. However, the   + 1, 0
fact that two measures are correlated does not necessarily mean that

one _____ the other.   causes

self-test

_____ 1. A psychologist who emphasized statistical analysis of measures was
   a. Galton
   b. Wundt
   c. James
   d. Watson

_____ 2. The assignment of numbers to traits, events, or objects according to some kind of orderly system is called
   a. statistics
   b. the statistical method
   c. measurement
   d. ordinal scaling

_____ 3. The application of mathematical principles to the interpretation of measurements is called
   a. measurement analysis
   b. probability
   c. sampling
   d. the statistical method

_____ 4. Temperature in degrees is an example of a(n)
   a. interval scale
   b. ratio scale
   c. nominal scale
   d. ordinal scale

_____ 5. The numbers on football players' backs form a(n)
   a. ordinal scale
   b. interval scale
   c. nominal scale
   d. ratio scale

_____ 6. The normal curve of distribution is
   a. humped in the middle and at one end
   b. symmetrical and bell-shaped
   c. flat in the middle and humped on the ends
   d. a straight line

_____ 7. Which distribution is most likely to be normal?
   a. the weights of boys in a given high school class
   b. the ages of children in a given grade school
   c. the ages of cars passing on a given street corner
   d. the ages at which girls marry

_____ 8. Mean, median, and mode are all
   a. inferential statistics
   b. measures of variability of scores
   c. measures of central tendency
   d. types of percentiles

_____ 9. The point below which 50 percent of the scores fall is the
   a. mean
   b. median
   c. mode
   d. 49th percentile

_____ 10. A measure of variability is the
   a. percentile
   b. standard deviation
   c. mode
   d. randomness index

_____11. A statistical index that helps to give meaning to a single score in a group of scores is the
a. mean
b. standard deviation
c. percentile
d. standard error of a score

_____12. In a normal distribution of scores with a mean of 100 and a standard deviation of 10, a score of 121 would be at about what percentile?
a. 5th
b. 20th
c. 70th
d. 98th

_____13. In inferential statistics we make generalizations from
a. sample to population
b. population to sample
c. population to universe
d. universe to population

_____14. A subgroup for which every element in the larger group had an equal opportunity to be selected is called a
a. normal sample
b. random sample
c. random population
d. universe

_____15. The purpose of a control group is to
a. maintain tighter control over the experimental treatment
b. increase the size of the sample
c. have two different groups of subjects getting the same treatment so as to have two independent sources of data on the same variable
d. determine if the effects observed in the experimental group were caused by factors other than the one being studied

_____16. The variability of a mean is usually measured by the
a. mode
b. standard error of the mean
c. range of the mean
d. standard error of the difference between two means

_____17. A test of significance of the difference between means determines the probability that the
a. results of the experiment are valid
b. experimental manipulation caused the difference in observed behavior
c. distribution was normal
d. observed difference in behavior between the groups was merely a function of chance factors

_____18. The correlation coefficient can take on values between
a. 0 and 100
b. 0 and +1
c. −1 and 0
d. −1 and +1

_____19. One method of assessing a correlation without computing it is to examine a
a. list of the numbers
b. population
c. scatter plot
d. normal distribution of dots

_____20. Although height and weight are found to have a correlation of .80 in a group of elementary school children, there may not really be a cause and effect relationship between height and weight because the
a. two may be correlated only because they both increase with age
b. correlation is only approximate
c. square of the correlation coefficient is only .64
d. measurements are not valid

Key to Self-Test

1. (a); 2. (c); 3. (d); 4. (a); 5. (c); 6. (b); 7. (a); 8. (c); 9. (b); 10. (b); 11. (c); 12. (d); 13. (a); 14. (b); 15. (d); 16. (b); 17. (d); 18. (d); 19. (c); 20. (a)

exercises

I. The curves in Figure 13–1 have the same mean score, median, and mode but differ in one important respect. Discuss the nature of this difference and describe the numerical index statisticians use to measure this characteristic of distributions. Explain why the index is an appropriate measure of this characteristic.

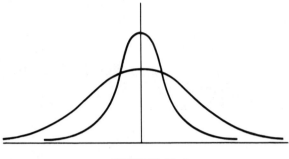

FIGURE 13–1

II. Below is a pair of scores for each of thirteen subjects. The first score (X) is for an intelligence test given at the beginning of kindergarten, and the second score (Y) is for an achievement test given near the end of the year. Find the mean, median, mode, and SD of the X- and Y-scores separately; then find the correlation coefficient of the two sets of scores.

Subject	X	Y
1	1	2
2	7	8
3	3	1
4	5	1
5	8	3
6	1	1
7	4	7
8	9	6
9	8	5
10	3	7
11	7	2
12	3	4
13	9	9

III. The scores listed below are the results of an experiment in which two groups of rats were tested in a maze-learning task. A high score represents a good performance. Group A received a drug before the testing; group B did not. Compute the critical ratio for the two groups. If the ratio is greater than 2.06 the probability is less than .05 that the observed difference in the means of the two groups is merely a function of chance factors associated with sampling. Interpret the results in light of this information.

Group A	Group B
7	4
6	1
8	3
9	8
3	5
1	4
7	2
10	2

CHAPTER 14

MEASURING INTELLIGENCE AND PERSONALITY

programed unit

1. Psychological *tests* attempt to measure intelligence, other aptitudes, achievement in school work and other skills, and personality traits. The Stanford-Binet Intelligence Scale, which measures intelligence, is an example of a psychological _____.

test

2. Since it is impossible to measure all the different ways in which a person might display intelligence or personality traits, a psychological test must rely on a limited *sample of behavior*. Thus the Stanford-Binet Intelligence Scale measures only some of the ways in which a person might display intelligence; that is, it measures a _____ of his behavior.

sample

3. A device that attempts to make a scientific measurement of a sample of behavior is a psychological _____.

test

4. From the sample of behavior measured in a psychological test, it is often possible to *predict* future behavior. The Scholastic Aptitude Tests help _____ a student's success in college.

predict

5. A psychological test often can predict a person's future behavior by measuring a _____ of his present behavior.

sample

6. Psychological tests should meet four strict requirements, insofar as possible. First, the test should be *objective*. In demanding that the test results be uncolored by the personal opinions or prejudices of the person who gives and grades the test—so that any qualified person can use the test in the same way and obtain the same results—the psychologist is saying that a test should be _____.

objective

7. The test should also be *standardized* by being administered to large

numbers of people, so that an individual's score can be compared with the scores of others and seen to be high, average, or low. A test that has been pretested on many people is said to be _____.   standardized

8. An individual's score on a psychological test can be seen to be high, average, or low if the test has been _____.   standardized

9. A test should also be *reliable;* that is, the scores it yields must be consistent. If an individual makes approximately the same score on a test on two different occasions, some time apart, the test probably meets the requirement of being _____.   reliable

10. If a person makes approximately the same score on the odd-numbered items of the test as on the even-numbered items, this is also an indication that the test is _____.   reliable

11. Finally, a test should be *valid;* it should actually measure what it is supposed to measure. The psychologist must make sure, in one way or another, that a test for aptitude in music actually measures musical ability rather than reading skill and is therefore _____.   valid

12. *Review*
    a. A psychological test is a scientific effort to measure a _____ of behavior.   sample
    b. The results of a psychological test are often used successfully to _____ future behavior.   predict
    c. If any qualified person can give and score the test in the same way and obtain the same results, uncolored by his own opinions or prejudices, the test meets the requirement of being _____.   objective
    d. If the test has been administered to large numbers of people, so that an individual's score can be compared with the scores of others and seen to be high, average, or low, the test meets the requirement of being _____.   standardized
    e. If an individual makes approximately the same score on the odd-numbered items of a test as on the even-numbered items, or on the entire test when he takes it on two different occasions, the test probably meets the requirement of being _____.   reliable
    f. If the test actually measures what it is supposed to measure, it meets the requirement of being _____.   valid

13. A *group test* can be administered to many people at once. A printed intelligence test that can be passed out in a classroom, so that all the

students can work on it and write in their answers at the same time, is

a _____ test.   group

14. An *individual test* can be given to only one person at a time. The Stanford-Binet Intelligence Scale, which requires the examiner to ask his

subject for verbal answers or to perform certain tasks, is an _____   individual
test.

15. An *aptitude test* attempts to measure a person's capacity to learn a new
skill. An intelligence test, which attempts to measure a person's ability

to learn new skills in school, is an _____ test.   aptitude

16. An *achievement test* measures the individual's present level of skill—
that is, how much he has already learned. The Iowa and Stanford tests,
which measure a person's performance in such subjects as reading and

arithmetic, are _____ tests.   achievement

17. A test that measures the individual's capacity to perform in the future

is an _____ test; a test that measures his present ability   aptitude

to perform is an _____ test.   achievement

18. *Review*
  a. A test that can be administered to many people at once is a _____   group
  test.
  b. A test that must be administered to one person at a time is an

  _____ test.   individual

  c. A test that measures a person's capacity to learn a new skill is an

  _____ test.   aptitude

  d. A test that measures a person's present level of skill is an _____ achievement
  test.

19. *Mental age* is the child's level of development as shown by his score on
an intelligence test. A child who scores as well as the average six-year-

old has a _____ _____ of six.   mental age

20. Mental age may be the same as or different from *chronological age,* which
is the child's age in years and months. A child celebrating his sixth birth-

day has a _____ _____ of six.   chronological age

21. The *intelligence quotient,* or *I.Q.,* is the child's mental age divided by his
chronological age, then multiplied by 100. If a child of six also has a

mental age of six, the formula $\dfrac{6}{6} \times 100$ works out to 100, which is his

_____ _____.   intelligence quotient

22. If a child of six (72 months) has a mental age of six years and eight months (80 months), the formula $\dfrac{80}{72} \times 100$ works out to 111, which is

his _____ _____ .   intelligence quotient

23. I.Q. can also be determined by comparing an individual's score on an intelligence test with the scores made by a large *standardization* group of others who have taken the test. If a person makes a raw score of 136 on a certain intelligence test, and 136 is the average raw score made by a

_____ group, his I.Q. is 100.   standardization

24. An intelligence quotient of 100 is average. The person with an I.Q. of

111 is _____ average.   above

25. The person with an I.Q. of less than 100 is _____ average.   below

26. Intelligence tests establishing an individual's I.Q. were originally designed to *predict* success in school and this is still perhaps their chief

value. If a child has an I.Q. of 111, we can _____ that he is   predict
likely to do well in school.

27. A weakness of intelligence tests is that they contain a *bias* in favor of people who have grown up in environments where they have had an opportunity to acquire the kinds of knowledge and language abilities that are typical of the middle and upper classes. The fact that children from middle-class and upper-class homes make higher scores than children from lower-class homes, and city children higher scores than

rural children, is at least partly due to the _____ contained in   bias
intelligence tests.

28. *Review*
    a. A child's level of intellectual development as shown by his score on an

    intelligence test is his _____ _____ .   mental age
    b. The intelligence quotient, or I.Q., is obtained by dividing the child's

    mental age by his _____ _____ and   chronological age
    then multiplying by 100.
    c. I.Q. can also be obtained by comparing the individual's raw score on an

    intelligence test with the scores made by a _____   standardization
    group.

    d. An I.Q. of more than 100 is _____ average; an I.Q. of less   above

    than 100 is _____ average.   below

    e. Intelligence tests and I.Q. are especially useful in helping _____   predict
    success in school.

f. A weakness of intelligence tests is that they contain a _____ in favor of those who have grown up in middle-class or upper-class environments.

bias

29. *Heredity* is one factor that may determine I.Q., as is shown by the fact that identical twins reared in the same home show a correlation of .92 in I.Q.'s — a mathematical expression for a very high degree of similarity. Since identical twins inherit exactly the same chromosomes and genes, this high correlation suggests that I.Q. depends at least in part on

_____.

heredity

30. *Environment* also helps determine I.Q., as is shown by the fact that for identical twins reared in different homes the correlation between I.Q.'s drops to .84. If two people with exactly the same heredity show a difference in I.Q.'s,

the difference must be due to _____.

environment

31. A study of children moved from a crowded orphanage into a less crowded home for the retarded where an affectionate and homelike atmosphere was provided showed an average increase in I.Q. from 64 to

92. This study also demonstrates that _____ helps determine I.Q.

environment

32. One investigator has suggested that a person with an unusually favorable pattern of genes may show an I.Q. over 150 if he grows up in the most stimulating possible environment but as low as 65 if his intellectual development is thwarted. This estimate stresses the importance

of both _____ and _____ in determining I.Q.

heredity, environment

33. The *mentally retarded* are those with an I.Q. under 70. A person with an

I.Q. of 60 is _____ _____.

mentally retarded

34. The *mentally gifted* are those with an I.Q. over 130. A person with an

I.Q. of 140 is _____ _____.

mentally gifted

35. *Review*
   a. The high correlation between I.Q.'s of identical twins reared in the same

   home suggests that I.Q. is determined partly by _____.

   heredity

   b. The lower correlation between I.Q.'s of identical twins reared in different homes suggests that I.Q. is determined partly by

   _____.

   environment

   c. A person with an I.Q. under 70 is _____

   _____.

   mentally

   retarded

   d. A person with an I.Q. over 130 is _____ _____.

   mentally gifted

36. *Vocational aptitude tests* measure an individual's capacity to perform the skills required by various kinds of jobs. A test for motor coordination required to operate complicated industrial machinery is a

  _____ _____ test.   vocational aptitude

37. *Interest tests* measure the individual's degree of interest in such matters as school subjects, social activities, and leisure activities. A test designed to show whether a person enjoys social gatherings more than

  going to football games is an _____ test.   interest

38. *Personality tests* measure the various traits that go to make up personality. A test that attempts to measure whether a person is normal or

  neurotic is one kind of _____ test.   personality

39. An *objective* personality test is one that is administered and scored according to a standard procedure, producing scores not seriously affected by the opinions or prejudices of the examiner. The Minnesota Multiphasic Personality Inventory (or MMPI), a true-or-false test that can be scored by an examiner who has not even seen the person taking it, is

  an _____ personality test.   objective

40. In a *situational test* of personality, the examiner observes the behavior of the subject in a situation deliberately designed to bring out certain aspects of his personality. A stress interview, in which the examiner asks questions that are deliberately hostile and pretends to disbelieve the

  answers, is a _____ test of personality.   situational

41. In a *projective test* of personality, the subject is asked to describe or make up a story about ambiguous designs or pictures; the theory is that the subject will project some of his own personality traits into his interpretations. The Thematic Apperception Test (or TAT), in which the subject is asked to make up stories about a set of drawings, is a

  _____ test of personality.   projective

42. *Review*
  a. A test that measures an individual's capacity for the skills required by

    various kinds of jobs is a _____ _____   vocational aptitude
    test.
  b. A test that measures an individual's degree of interest in such matters as school subjects, social activities, and leisure activities is an

    _____ test.   interest
  c. A test that measures the various traits that go to make up personality

    is a _____ test.   personality
  d. A personality test that is administered and scored according to a standard procedure, producing scores not seriously affected by the opin-

ions or prejudices of the examiner, is an _____ objective
personality test.

e. A test in which the examiner observes the behavior of the subject in a situation deliberately designed to bring out certain aspects of his

personality is a _____ personality test. situational

f. A test in which the subject is asked to describe or make up stories

about ambiguous designs or pictures is a _____ projective
personality test.

self-test

_____ 1. A psychological test on which the subject gets the same score regardless of who administers and grades it meets the requirement of
a. objectivity
b. standardization
c. reliability
d. validity

_____ 2. If a person makes approximately the same score on the odd-numbered items as on the even-numbered items, the test probably meets the requirement of
a. objectivity
b. standardization
c. reliability
d. validity

_____ 3. A test meets the requirement of validity if it
a. gives consistent scores
b. can be administered by anyone
c. gives approximately the same scores when taken by a person on two different occasions
d. actually measures what it is intended to measure

_____ 4. A test that can be taken by many persons at the same time and gives a score indicating capacity to learn a new skill is a(n)
a. individual test of aptitude
b. individual test of achievement

c. group test of aptitude
d. group test of achievement

_____ 5. The Stanford-Binet is a(n)
a. individual test of intelligence
b. group test of personality
c. individual test of vocational aptitude
d. group test of interests

_____ 6. The division of items into two categories, verbal and performance, is the distinguishing feature of the
a. Stanford-Binet tests
b. Wechsler tests
c. Pintner-Cunningham Primary Test
d. Armed Forces Qualification Test

_____ 7. Intelligence tests are *not*
a. objective
b. standardized
c. reliable
d. unbiased

_____ 8. Intelligence tests are most useful in
a. predicting success in school
b. predicting a person's ability to adjust
c. predicting a person's future income
d. measuring basic intelligence

_____ 9. The correlation between I.Q.'s of identical twins reared in the same home is
a. .30

b. .50

c. .84

d. .92

_____10. The correlation between I.Q.'s of identical twins reared in different homes is

a. .30

b. .50

c. .84

d. .92

_____11. The prevailing view of psychologists is that heredity

a. has no effect on I.Q.

b. is the chief factor in determining I.Q.

c. sets a top and bottom limit on the individual's I.Q. score

d. none of the above

_____12. Even among children who continue to live in the same home and therefore much the same environment, tests of the same individuals over a period of years have shown

a. a steady rise in I.Q.

b. a tendency for girls' I.Q. to rise

c. a tendency for boys' I.Q. to fall

d. upward or downward changes of as much as 50 points in I.Q.

_____13. When the Wechsler test is given to individuals of different ages, the results indicate that

a. the average total score declines sharply after the age of twenty-four

b. ability at verbal skills remains fairly constant through the age of forty-four, then declines slowly

c. ability at verbal skills declines faster than ability on performance tasks

d. scores do not reach their peak until about the age of thirty-four

_____14. Intelligence tests of men in different occupations show that

a. there is no relation between I.Q. and job

b. the highest average I.Q. is found among teachers

c. a wide range of I.Q.'s is found in every occupation

d. the average I.Q. of lawyers and engineers is higher than the I.Q. of any farmhand or miner

_____15. Which of the following has *not* been found to be a cause of mental retardation?

a. having a retarded brother or sister

b. Mongolism

c. cretinism

d. German measles suffered by the mother during pregnancy

_____16. A long-term study of mentally gifted children has shown that

a. they were below average in height and weight

b. they were less well adjusted than average

c. on the whole, they were outstandingly successful as adults

d. none of them turned out to be a vocational misfit or drifter

_____17. The Kuder Preference Record is a(n)

a. vocational aptitude test

b. interest test

c. objective test of personality

d. projective test of personality

_____18. The MMPI is a(n)

a. vocational aptitude test

b. interest test

c. objective test of personality

d. projective test of personality

_____19. When a psychologist conducts an interview in which he deliberately causes stress by asking hostile questions and pretending to disbelieve the answers, he is giving a(n)

a. Rorschach test

b. objective test of personality

c. situational test of personality

d. projective test of personality

_____20. The Thematic Apperception Test (TAT) is a(n)
    a. vocational aptitude test
    b. interest test
    c. objective test of personality
    d. projective test of personality

exercise

A factor that is measured by some intelligence tests and that is closely related to one of the skills measured by all such tests is memory span for digits. Thus a simple test of memory span for digits provides a quick demonstration of how mental ability rapidly increases with age up to the late teens. If you try the following series of digits on children of various ages and on some of your classmates, you will doubtless find some substantial differences. The number of digits that can be recalled perfectly depends in part on how fast they are read to the subject—but if you read them at the rate of about one digit a second, you will probably find that the average young child can recall a series of about four, an older child about five or six, a college student six or seven or even more. (Individual differences, of course, play a large part.)

Start with the shortest of the series and continue until your subject is unable to call the series back without error. Usually the dividing line is quite distinct; you will find, for example, that some subjects can recall a series of five perfectly every time but lose track completely when the number of digits is increased to six.

Series of three:	8, 5, 2
	7, 9, 3
	2, 7, 1
Series of four:	1, 9, 7, 3
	8, 2, 1, 6
	9, 4, 7, 5
Series of five:	3, 7, 9, 2, 5
	6, 1, 4, 9, 3
	2, 8, 3, 5, 7
Series of six:	9, 3, 6, 8, 5, 2
	8, 1, 9, 4, 7, 5
	2, 8, 4, 7, 3, 6
Series of seven:	4, 9, 3, 7, 2, 1, 6
	5, 3, 1, 8, 2, 7, 4
	6, 2, 9, 5, 3, 8, 7
Series of eight:	1, 4, 8, 3, 9, 6, 2, 7
	5, 2, 9, 6, 3, 7, 4, 8
	9, 2, 7, 3, 4, 8, 5, 2
Series of nine:	7, 1, 8, 5, 2, 6, 3, 9, 4
	2, 9, 6, 4, 7, 3, 5, 8, 1
	4, 1, 8, 2, 9, 5, 3, 7, 6

CHAPTER 15

developmental psychology

programed unit

1. *Developmental psychology* is the study of the processes by which the child gradually acquires his adult patterns of behavior, thinking, and personality. Because adult personality has its roots in childhood it is virtually impossible to understand adult behavior without knowing

   something about _____ _____.

   developmental psychology

2. When found in established form among adults, many psychological problems (crime, alcoholism, psychosis) are difficult to treat. But we may learn to prevent them or deal with them successfully in their early

   stages through the study of _____

   _____.

   developmental

   psychology

3. Developmental psychology has found that babies exhibit a number of *inborn* individual differences. Since babies show these individual differences at or shortly after birth, we know that the differences are

   _____.

   inborn

4. Among the inborn individual differences are differences in *level of activity*. The fact that some children move with considerable force, sleep restlessly, and suck vigorously when nursing, whereas others are more

   placid and quiet, indicates individual differences in _____

   ___ _____.

   level

   of activity

5. Boy babies tend to be more vigorous and restless than girl babies. The

   two sexes appear to show an inborn difference in _____

   ___ _____.

   level

   of activity

6. Individual differences also exist in *sensory thresholds* and *adaptation*. The fact that some babies respond to very mild stimuli and are slow to

164

adapt to stimuli, whereas others respond only to stronger stimuli and are quick to adapt to them, indicates inborn differences in sensory

_____ and _____.   thresholds, adaptation

7. *Irritability* is another trait in which babies show individual differences. A baby who begins to fret, whine, or cry at the slightest provocation is

high in _____.   irritability

8. A baby who does not fret or cry unless his discomfort or pain is quite

intense is low in _____.   irritability

9. On the matter of temperament, about 40 percent of babies appear to be *"easy" children,* who are quite regular in eating and sleeping habits, generally cheerful, and quick to adapt to new schedules, foods, and people. In temperament, children who learn quickly to accept a bottle in

place of the breast are _____ _____.   "easy" children

10. About 15 percent of babies are classified as *"slow to warm up";* these babies tend to withdraw from their first exposure to a new experience, seem to be somewhat negative in mood, and display a low level of activity. A baby who rejects the bottle the first time it is offered may be clas-

sified as _____ ____ _____ _____.   "slow to warm up"

11. Another 10 percent of babies are *"difficult" children.* Babies who are irregular in sleeping and eating habits, very slow in adjusting to new experiences, quite negative in mood, and given to unusually intense re-

actions, such as loud crying and temper tantrums, are _____   "difficult"

_____.   children

12. *Mixed types* in temperament show some of the characteristics of all the others. The approximately 35 percent of babies who cannot be clas-

sified as either "easy," "slow to warm up," or "difficult" are _____   mixed

_____.   types

13. The study of inborn individual differences has indicated that each infant is an individual who requires *individual treatment* if he is to attain his maximum potential. Rather than treating "easy" and "difficult" children exactly alike, parents and teachers should give them

_____ treatment, differing from child to child.   individual

14. *Review*
    a. The study of how children acquire their adult patterns of behavior,

    thinking, and personality is _____   developmental

    _____.   psychology

b. Developmental psychology's study of babies at or shortly after birth has shown that they display various _____ individual differences. — inborn

c. Among inborn individual differences are differences in vigor and restlessness, called _____ _____ _____. — level of activity

d. The fact that some children respond to weaker stimuli and adapt more slowly than others points to inborn individual differences in sensory _____ and _____. — thresholds, adaptation

e. The fact that some babies fret or cry at the slightest provocation, and others only when their discomfort or pain is intense points to inborn individual differences in _____. — irritability

f. In temperament, babies fall into three distinctive classifications: those who are regular in eating and sleeping habits, generally cheerful, and quick to adapt are called _____ _____; — "easy" children
those who tend to withdraw from their first exposure to a new experience, seem somewhat negative in mood, and display a low level of activity are _____ _____ _____ _____; and those — "slow to warm up"
who are irregular in eating and sleeping habits, slow in adjusting to new experiences, quite negative in mood, and given to unusually intense reactions are called _____ _____. — "difficult" children

g. Babies who show some of the characteristics of all the types and cannot be placed in any of the three classifications are _____ — mixed
_____. — types

15. *Maturation* is the process in which physical changes that take place after birth continue the development of the organism from fertilized egg cell to complete adult. Learning to sit alone and to walk is impossible until the necessary muscular and nervous structures have been provided by _____. — maturation

16. Maturation also aids in the development of *perception* and *language skills*. But increasing ability in perception and language also depends to a great extent on *learning*. The fact that a baby at the age of about four months is likely to smile when he sees a human face is due not only to maturation but also to _____. — learning

17. As the child grows older, his perceptual processes improve in many ways. He becomes efficient at scanning a stimulus, attending to the distinctive features, extracting information, and comparing the information with his previous experiences. Much of his increased skill is the result of _____. — learning

18. The fact that children who grow up in stimulating environments de-

velop language skills more rapidly than children brought up in the deprived atmosphere of orphanages indicates that the development of language skills depends to a great extent on _____.

learning

19. Thus learning is important in the development of both _____ and _____ skills.

perception

language

20. *Intellectual development* proceeds in an orderly and predictable manner, partly through maturation and partly through learning—especially the learning of concepts. The child's increasing ability to think and solve problems is an indication of his _____ _____.

intellectual

development

21. The Swiss psychologist *Piaget* has defined intellectual development as basically an increased ability to adapt to new situations. The child's increasing ability to adapt to new situations as represented by new kinds of problems to solve is the basic mark of intellectual development according to _____.

Piaget

22. One of two key processes in intellectual development, according to Piaget, is *assimilation,* the process of incorporating a new stimulus into one's existing view of the world. When a child first encounters a toy magnet and tries to incorporate it into his view of toys by banging it like a hammer or throwing it like a ball, he is demonstrating the process called _____.

assimilation

23. The other key process in intellectual development, according to Piaget, is *accommodation*—or changing one's view and behavior when new information dictates such a change. When the child learns that a toy magnet can attract metal and changes his view of toys to take account of the fact that some toys are not to bang or throw but to attract metal, he is demonstrating the process called _____.

accommodation

24. According to Piaget, intellectual development through assimilation and accommodation takes place in four *stages,* in each of which the child thinks and behaves in quite different fashion from before. Thus Piaget's theory outlines four _____ of intellectual development.

stages

25. *Sensorimotor stage* is the name given by Piaget to the first stage of intellectual development, birth to age two. Because the child at this stage has not yet learned to use symbols and language and is dependent on the raw evidence of his senses and motor movements (bodily actions), this first stage is known as the _____ stage.

sensorimotor

26. *Stage of formal operations* is the name given by Piaget to the final stage of intellectual development, beginning at about eleven or twelve. The

ability to think in the abstract like an adult is characteristic of the stage

of _____ _____.   formal operations

27. *Review*

   a. The process in which physical changes that take place after birth
continue the development of the organism from fertilized egg cell to

     complete adult is _____.   maturation

   b. Although maturation plays a key role in the development of such
physical skills as sitting alone and walking, the development of
skills in perception and language depends not only on maturation

     but also on _____.   learning

   c. The child's increasing ability to think and solve problems is an

     indication of his _____ development.   intellectual

   d. According to Piaget, the key processes in intellectual development

     are _____ and _____.   assimilation,
                                   accommodation

   e. Piaget also contributed the theory that intellectual development takes

     place in a series of four _____.   stages

   f. The stage from birth to age two, when the child is dependent on the
raw evidence of his senses and motor movements, is termed by

     Piaget the _____ stage.   sensorimotor

   g. The fourth stage, beginning at about eleven or twelve when the
child becomes capable of thinking in the abstract like an adult, is

     termed by Piaget the stage of _____ _____. formal operations

28. Personality development begins with the *caretaker period,* from birth to
eighteen months. Because the child has such a close relationship at
this time with his mother or another adult who nurtures him, this is

   called the _____ period.   caretaker

29. The *theory of attachment* holds that the baby inherits a strong tendency
to become attached to another person, usually the mother. The baby's
inherited tendencies to root, suck, babble, smile, and cry—all of which
are directed toward stimuli that can only be provided by another per-

   son—are the basis of the theory of _____.   attachment

30. The theory of attachment is one explanation of personality develop-

   ment during the _____ period.   caretaker

31. A different theory holds that the child's close relationship with the
caretaker results from her *"reward value."* Because the mother or caretaker relieves hunger and pain and provides comfort, she acquires

   _____ _____.   "reward value"

32. *Separation anxiety,* in response to being left by the mother or care-

taker, first occurs during the caretaker period. Since the baby cannot understand or explain the caretaker's disappearance, he exhibits

_____ _____.   separation anxiety

33. *Stranger anxiety* also appears during the caretaker period. Because the appearance of someone other than the caretaker generates uncertainty,

the child displays _____ _____.   stranger anxiety

34. *Review*
    a. The period from birth to eighteen months, when the child's personality development depends on his close relationship with his

    mother or other nurturing person, is the _____   caretaker

    _____.   period

    b. The theory that the baby inherits a strong tendency to become attached to another person, usually the mother, is the theory of

    _____.   attachment

    c. A different theory holds that the baby's close relationship with his

    mother results from her _____ _____ as a   "reward value"
    provider of food and comfort.
    d. The caretaker period is marked by the appearance of two forms of

    anxiety — _____ anxiety and _____   separation, stranger
    anxiety.

35. The period from eighteen months through three years is characterized by the *first social demands* on the child. Being asked to conform to discipline and undergo toilet training introduces the child to his first

_____ _____.   social demands

36. Too much discipline or protection during the period from eighteen months through three years may instill a crippling amount of anxiety and create lifelong inhibitions against trying anything new or challenging. Thus a proper mixture of discipline and permissiveness is of

critical importance during the period of first _____   social

_____.   demands

37. The *preschool years,* four and five, are characterized by identification with the parents, development of standards, and the first notions of sex typing and conduct appropriate to males and females. The child is likely to begin thinking of himself as a boy or a girl during

the _____ _____.   preschool years

38. Feelings of guilt and a conscience, which depend on inner standards,

also develop during the _____ _____.   preschool years

39. At ages six to ten, the child's personality development comes under

the strong influence of his *peers*—that is, boys and girls of the same age. The child becomes less concerned with the opinions of his parents

than with the opinions of his _____.
            peers

40. A child's peers are important for purposes of *evaluation*. Since the child can see for himself whether other children regard him as competent and likable or foolish and unpleasant, they help him make an

_____ of himself.
            evaluation

41. Peers also assign the child to a *role*. They may place him in the _____ of leader or follower, bright child or clown.
            role

42. Finally, peers provide an opportunity for *rebellion*. In the company of his peers the child can express his hostilities, be messy and noisy, and do

other things that constitute _____ against the restrictions of the adult world.
            rebellion

43. *Review*

   a. The period from eighteen months through three years is characterized by the first _____ _____ on the child.
            social demands

   b. The years four and five, when the child identifies with his parents and develops standards and notions of sex typing, are the

_____ years.
            preschool

   c. At ages six to ten, the child's personality development comes under

the strong influence of his _____.
            peers

   d. By regarding him as competent or foolish, likable or unpleasant, the

child's peers help him make an _____ of himself.
            evaluation

   e. His peers also assign the child to a _____, as of leader or follower, bright child or clown.
            role

   f. His peers also provide an opportunity for _____ against the restrictions of the adult world.
            rebellion

self-test

_____ 1. Babies are sensitive to stimuli in their environments and can make reflex responses to the stimuli
   a. from the moment of birth
   b. after two days
   c. after two weeks
   d. after two months

_____ 2. Newborn babies show the least dra-matic individual differences in which one of the following?
   a. level of activity
   b. sensory thresholds and adaptation
   c. irritability
   d. rooting response

_____ 3. A child who tends to withdraw from his first exposure to a new experience,

is somewhat negative in mood, and displays a low level of activity is classed as
a. "easy"
b. "slow to warm up"
c. "difficult"
d. a mixed type

_____ 4. Findings of differences in temperament among babies have indicated that the child needs
a. strict discipline
b. coaxing
c. permissive treatment
d. individual treatment

_____ 5. The child's increasing skill at using his muscles is due chiefly to
a. maturation
b. learning
c. "pushing" by his parents
d. an opportunity to exercise

_____ 6. The first language skill the infant develops is
a. use of phonemes
b. use of morphemes
c. expression
d. comprehension

_____ 7. In intellectual development, Piaget's term for the process of incorporating a new stimulus into one's view of the world is
a. accommodation
b. assimilation
c. intuitive understanding
d. conservation

_____ 8. The ability to use symbols and language begins to dominate intellectual development during Piaget's
a. sensorimotor stage
b. preoperational stage
c. stage of concrete operations
d. stage of formal operations

_____ 9. The child learns the principle of conservation during Piaget's
a. sensorimotor stage
b. preoperational stage
c. stage of concrete operations
d. stage of formal operations

_____ 10. The theory of attachment emphasizes
a. learning
b. inherited responses
c. the mother's "reward value"
d. maturation

_____ 11. A young child is likely to show greater tendencies to explore his environment if he is
a. alone
b. in the company of a stranger
c. with his mother
d. with other children

_____ 12. The child first displays anxiety
a. during the caretaker period
b. at about the age of two
c. when he encounters the first social demands
d. in the preschool years

_____ 13. Children who spend the caretaker period in an orphanage are likely to display all but which of the following when they are older?
a. independence
b. aggressiveness
c. temper tantrums
d. difficulty in forming affectionate personal relationships

_____ 14. Conscience develops most rapidly during the
a. caretaker period
b. period of first social demands
c. preschool years
d. ages six to ten

_____ 15. Many children develop a pronounced fear of failure
a. during the caretaker period
b. during the preschool years
c. because of inherited temperament
d. because of experiences in school

_____ 16. The chief influences in assigning the child a role are his
a. parents

b. teachers
c. peers
d. experiences in school

_____17. Children in the Soviet Union, in contrast to American children, have been found less inclined to perform forbidden acts if told that their actions will be made known to
a. the experimenters
b. their parents
c. their classmates
d. no one

_____18. Children are likely to develop tendencies to be dominant if they
a. have dominant parents
b. have permissive parents
c. are disliked by their classmates
d. are physically weak or unattractive

_____19. The child begins to acquire a motive

for cognitive consonance in the
a. caretaker period
b. period of first social demands
c. preschool period
d. early school years

_____20. The child's personality at age ten
a. is undergoing rapid changes
b. is too undeveloped to measure
c. will change drastically during adolescence
d. is a reasonably accurate preview of what he will be like as an adult

Key to Self-Test

1. (a); 2. (d); 3. (b); 4. (d); 5. (a); 6. (d); 7. (b); 8. (b); 9. (c); 10. (b); 11. (c); 12. (a); 13. (a); 14. (c); 15. (d); 16. (c); 17. (c); 18. (b); 19. (d); 20. (d)

exercise

On page 173 is a set of drawings that can be used to perform your own version of the experiment described in the textbook on pages 529–30.* The experiment provides a striking demonstration of how children, as they develop intellectually, make an increasing use of concepts and categories in coding and retrieval.

Note that the twenty-four drawings fall into four categories; all those in column 1 are means of transportation, in 2 animals, in 3 furniture, and in 4 clothing. The question the experiment attempts to answer is at what ages and to what extent children begin to utilize these categories when asked to study and remember the pictures.

For an informal version of the original experiment, all that is needed is the drawings and one college-age subject, plus some children from as many of the elementary grades as possible. Cut

out the drawings along the lines, so that each is a separate square—and, if you want to make them more durable, attach them to pieces of cardboard with transparent tape.

Testing each subject individually, show him the twenty-four drawings one at a time in random order, asking him to tell you what each represents and correcting him if necessary (as may happen with younger children). Then tell him that you are going to put the drawings on a table or desk in front of him, let him study them for three minutes, and then see how many he remembers. Tell him also that during the three minutes he can do anything with the pictures that he thinks will help him remember them—for example, pick them up, move them around, or even take notes. In placing the drawings in front of him, mix them up so that he will have to discover the four categories for himself.

As each subject studies the drawings, make note of whether he attempts to organize them by categories. You can score him on a scale similar

*Neimark, E., Slotnick, N. S., and Ulrich, T. The development of memorization strategies. *Developmental Psychology*, 1971, *5*, 427–32.

   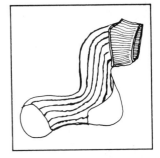

to the one devised by the psychologists who designed the experiment—0 if he makes no attempt at systematic arrangement, 1 if he organizes some but not all of the drawings into the appropriate groups or seems to arrange them into some kind of grouping of his own, 2 if he rearranges them into the four categories, and 3 if he not only arranges them into the categories but also attempts to make some kind of further organization within each category—such as putting train and truck together because they begin with the same letter of the alphabet.

At the end of the three minutes, remove the drawings and ask the subject to recall as many of them as he can. As he calls out the names he remembers, try to note whether he is recalling them in chunks of some kind—especially in chunks dictated by the four categories.

Although results with only a few subjects may be distorted by individual differences, your findings will almost surely show some strong evidence of an increasing tendency to use categories—and therefore to recall more of the drawings—with increasing age. Your college subject will almost surely rearrange the drawings into the four categories as he studies them and may very well also do some further rearranging within each category. A first-grader, on the other hand, will probably make no attempt to rearrange the drawings into categories; and he will probably be able to remember only about eight of them, in an order that does not indicate much if any chunking. Older children fall somewhere in between. (In the original experiment, third-graders recalled an average of about twelve drawings, fourth-graders fourteen, and sixth-graders sixteen. Their scores on the scales for using categories and chunking are shown in the graph on page 529 of the text.)

social psychology

programed unit

1. The study of how people influence and are influenced by other people is called *social psychology*. Thus an experiment that measures aggressive behavior in groups is an experiment in _____ psychology.

   social

2. The process by which the child is taught the customs and rules of his society is called *socialization*. Since the socialization process largely determines how the child will behave with others in society, it is an important topic in _____ psychology.

   social

3. As the child grows up, he learns from adults how he is expected to behave in society. This process is known as _____.

   socialization

4. An important part of the socialization process is the acquisition of *norms,* the standards and expectations shared by the members of a society that regulate almost all kinds of behavior. The standards that say we should drive on the right side of the road, eat with a knife and fork, and wear suitable clothing in public are all _____.

   norms

5. Although most societies have similar norms governing such extremely disruptive forms of behavior as murder and rape, other norms may vary rather widely from one society to another. Driving on the left side of the road is a _____ in England but not in the United States.

   norm

6. In society, each of us at any given moment occupies a particular place or niche, giving us more or less prestige among our fellow men. Social psychologists call this our *position* in society — determined by such factors as age, place in the family, occupation, and membership in various groups. An elderly physician occupies a different _____ in society than does a high school girl.

   position

7. Each person usually occupies several different positions. A woman may

   occupy the _____ of wife, mother, jobholder, and   positions
   club member.

8. From a person in a given position, society expects a certain kind of
   behavior; the person is expected to play what social psychologists call
   the *role* appropriate to that position. Thus a woman is expected to play

   one _____ as wife, another as mother, still another as jobholder.   role

9. The role that a person is expected to play depends on his _____   position
   in society.

10. A person in the position of college student is expected to play one kind

    of _____, his instructor a different _____.   role, role

11. *Review*
    a. The study of how people influence and are influenced by other

    people is called _____ _____.   social psychology
    b. The process by which the child is taught the customs and rules of

    his society is _____.   socialization
    c. An important part of the socialization process is the acquisition of
    the standards and expectations shared by the members of a society,

    called _____.   norms
    d. The place or niche that a person occupies in society is called his

    _____.   position

    e. Society expects a person in a given position to play an appropriate

    _____.   role

12. Among the interests of social psychology are the factors that influence
    the manner in which we are attracted to other people; this is the study
    of *interpersonal attraction.* If we like another person at first sight, we

    are exhibiting one aspect of _____   interpersonal

    _____.   attraction

13. We tend to like people whom we perceive as being similar to ourselves.

    Thus similarity plays a large part in _____   interpersonal

    _____.   attraction

14. We tend to like people who are similar in interests and personality, who
    are familiar and live or work nearby, and who reciprocate the feeling of
    liking. Thus similarity, familiarity, and reciprocal liking are all factors

    in _____ _____.   interpersonal attraction

15. The importance of first impressions is called the *halo effect,* meaning that our general impressions of another person are strongly colored by any one thing, good or bad, that we initially learn about him. If a person makes a witty remark the first time we meet him, we are likely to judge him as generally bright and interesting because of the _____ _____.

halo effect

16. The fact that first impressions influence our feelings toward another person, called the _____ _____, is an important factor in _____ _____.

halo effect
interpersonal attraction

17. If we know that a person is important or wealthy, this is likely to influence the amount of attraction that we feel toward him. This kind of first impression is another aspect of the _____ _____.

halo effect

18. Among the factors that create interpersonal attraction are similarities in *beliefs,* which are opinions about matters of fact or presumed fact. When we share the opinion that the world is round, we share a _____.

belief

19. More deep-seated and important than beliefs are *attitudes.* An attitude is distinguished from a belief or an opinion chiefly by the fact that it has an *emotional* component. Besides representing a cognitive opinion, an attitude is also _____.

emotional

20. The opinion that the world is round, which is merely cognitive, is a _____. Because a religious conviction involves strong emotional feelings, it is an _____.

belief
attitude

21. A person who holds an attitude (say about religion or civil rights) also has a predisposition to behave in a particular way toward the object or situation that is the center of his attitude. Thus a *behavioral predisposition* is also part of an _____.

attitude

22. In sum, an attitude represents a combination of opinion or _____, plus feelings or _____, plus a _____ predisposition.

belief
emotion, behavioral

23. *Review*
    a. The study of how people are attracted to other people is called the study of _____ _____.

interpersonal
attraction

    b. Similarity of interests and personality, familiarity, and reciprocal

liking all are factors that tend to produce _____   interpersonal
                                                                  attraction

_____.

   c. The fact that first impressions influence our general opinion of another person is called the _____ _____.   halo effect

   d. A cognitive opinion is a _____.   belief
   e. When a cognitive opinion is accompanied by emotional overtones
   and a predisposition to behave in a particular way, it becomes an

   _____.   attitude

24. The *search for consistency* is the term applied to a person's tendency
    to seek harmony among the beliefs, emotions, and behavior that make
    up his attitudes. If a person changes his beliefs, emotions, or be-
    havior—and thus an attitude—he is likely to do so in a search for

    _____.   consistency

25. Because of the tendency to search for consistency, an attitude may be
    changed by new information that affects the cognitive opinion or

    _____ on which it is partially based, events that affect the   belief

    feelings or _____ that accompany it, or changes in   emotions

    the individual's actions or _____.   behavior

26. A deliberate attempt to change attitudes through the transmission of
    information or appeals to emotion is called a *persuasive communication.*
    An attempt to persuade people to stop smoking by establishing fear of

    lung cancer is a _____ _____.   persuasive
                                                              communication

27. Unfortunately for those who seek to change attitudes, persuasive com-
    munications are hampered by *selective exposure,* which means that for
    various reasons they by and large reach those who are already per-
    suaded. The fact that an appeal to stop smoking often receives the
    most attention from those who have already stopped is an example of

    _____ _____.   selective exposure

28. A persuasive communication is likely to be more effective if it comes
    from a source of high *credibility.* An appeal to stop smoking from a
    noted lung surgeon is likely to be more effective than an appeal from a

    classmate because of the surgeon's high _____.   credibility

29. A *"fair" argument* also seems to be more effective in persuasive com-
    munication than a one-sided argument. To be most effective, the lung
    surgeon would have to present both sides of the question and thus offer

    a _____ _____.   "fair" argument

30. Review

    a. The tendency to seek harmony among the beliefs, emotions, and

    behavior that make up an attitude is called the search for _____.   consistency

    b. A deliberate attempt to change attitudes through the transmission of

    information or appeals to emotion is a _____   persuasive

    _____.   communication

    c. The fact that most persuasive communications by and large reach

    people who are already persuaded is known as _____   selective

    _____.   exposure

    d. Persuasive communications are usually most effective when they

    come from a source of high _____ who   credibility

    presents not a one-sided but a _____ argument.   "fair"

31. The forces that operate in a group to produce leaders and to bring about other alignments, decisions, and activities are called *group dynamics.* The fact that every group usually produces a leader can be attributed to

    _____ _____.   group dynamics

32. What happens in a group depends largely on its pattern of *communication*—that is, on who talks to whom and how much. Thus communi-

    cation plays an important part in _____ _____.   group dynamics

33. The fact that the most talkative member of a group is usually also its

    leader demonstrates the importance of _____   communication
    in group dynamics.

34. Three factors that seem to be of special importance in determining leaders are 1) activity in the group, including communication, 2) ability to perform the task with which the group is concerned, and 3) personal likability. Thus a very active and talkative member who is good at his

    job and is well liked is likely to become a _____.   leader

35. *Risky shift* is the term applied to the fact that people are usually more willing to undertake risks in decisions made in groups than in decisions made individually. When ordinarily conservative people decide in committee to take more chances than any one of them would have been

    likely to undertake alone, they are exhibiting _____ _____.   risky shift

36. When a mob engages in acts of violence and cruelty that its members might never even think of individually, the mob is probably displaying

    _____ _____.   risky shift

37. *Review*

    a. The forces that produce leaders and determine group activities and decisions are _____ _____.   group dynamics

    b. Group dynamics depend in large part on the group's pattern of _____.   communication

    c. A group member who is active and talkative, has high ability to perform the task with which the group is concerned, and is well liked is likely to become its _____.   leader

    d. The fact that people are more likely to undertake risks in group decisions than in individual decisions is called _____ _____.   risky shift

38. *Conformity* is the yielding by an individual to pressures from the group in which he finds himself. If an individual goes along with the group's opinion even though he may have other inclinations, he is exhibiting _____.   conformity

39. In an experiment in which subjects administered to others what they thought were painful and dangerous electric shocks at the urging of members of their group, the subjects were exhibiting _____.   conformity

40. Group *unanimity* tends to produce conformity. When an individual notes that everybody else in the group agrees on a course of action, he is likely to go along because of the force of group _____.   unanimity

41. The group's *credibility* is also important. If an individual has confidence in the group and regards its members as having high status and expert knowledge, he is more likely to conform because of the group's _____.   credibility

42. The group's *size* is also important; the more members it has, at least up to a point, the more conformity it is likely to produce. Thus, in addition to unanimity and credibility, the individual's tendency to conform is influenced by the _____ of the group.   size

43. *Review*

    a. The yielding by an individual to pressures from the group in which he finds himself is _____.   conformity

    b. The individual is most likely to conform if all the other members of the group agree and thus display group _____.   unanimity

    c. If the individual has confidence in the group and high regard for its members, he is more likely to conform because of the group's _____.   credibility

d. The more members a group has, at least up to a point, the more likely an individual member is to conform—indicating that conformity is also influenced by the _____ of the group.   size

self-test

_____ 1. In contrast to the United States, there are some societies in which two friends would never dream of competing against each other, as in games or athletic contests. A social psychologist would attribute this to differences in
a. physical environment
b. biological inheritance
c. social-class structure
d. socialization

_____ 2. Norms can best be described as
a. standards and expectations shared by the members of a society
b. rules of law
c. statistically normal behavior
d. universal rules of conduct

_____ 3. In contrast with lower-class families, upper- and middle-class families tend to be characterized by all but which one of the following?
a. the parents' sense of control over their own and their children's lives
b. stricter child-rearing practices
c. greater achievement motivation among the children
d. more education and income

_____ 4. Upwardly mobile people often encounter psychological problems chiefly because of
a. financial problems
b. job strain
c. unfamiliar norms
d. social snobbery

_____ 5. Age, place in the family, occupation, and membership in groups are important factors in determining the individual's
a. social class
b. role
c. position
d. leadership qualities

_____ 6. When society expects a physician to be conscientious, humane, and sympathetic, it is asking that he
a. occupy his proper position
b. play the appropriate role
c. become a father figure
d. set an example for others

_____ 7. "Love at first sight" is an example of what social psychologists call
a. interpersonal attraction
b. the halo effect
c. attitude change
d. persuasive communication

_____ 8. When we meet a person for the first time, which one of the following things is *not* likely to make him seem attractive?
a. the fact that we have seen his photograph many times
b. knowing that we will work with him
c. finding that he shares our attitudes on politics
d. believing that he seems rather cool toward us

_____ 9. The halo effect refers to
a. the importance of first impressions
b. a gradual increase in liking for another person
c. the tendency of a person good at

one thing to be good at others

d. an attractive kind of personality

_____10. An attitude includes all but which one of the following factors?

a. a cognitive belief

b. emotion

c. a behavioral predisposition

d. eagerness for change

_____11. The college experience is likely to have which one of the following effects on attitudes?

a. no significant change

b. no change until after the freshman year

c. an increase in the number of students who vote as their parents do

d. changes that tend to persist throughout life

_____12. What students of attitude change call the search for consistency is based on the motive for

a. achievement

b. affiliation

c. certainty

d. mastery

_____13. Which of the following is the best example of a persuasive communication?

a. a friend's request for a loan

b. a political candidate's speech

c. a coach's pep talk to his team

d. a newspaper story on tax problems

_____14. The effectiveness of persuasive communications is hampered by all but which one of the following?

a. the weakness of appeals to emotion

b. selective exposure

c. the difficulty of reaching a large audience

d. the individual's tendency to resist attitude change

_____15. The effectiveness of a persuasive communication is likely to be increased

under all but which one of the following circumstances?

a. It comes from a source of high credibility.

b. It presents a "fair" rather than a one-sided argument.

c. It appeals to the listener's motives and emotions.

d. The listener believes that the attitude he possesses is a part of human nature or his inborn dispositions.

_____16. The forces called group dynamics operate to produce all but which one of the following effects?

a. establish leaders

b. determine the group's activities

c. encourage less talkative members to speak up

d. determine the group's decisions

_____17. What happens in a group is mostly determined by

a. the number of members

b. the age of its leader

c. the reason it was formed

d. who talks to whom and how much

_____18. The "task specialist" type of leader

a. is the best-liked member of the group

b. rates higher in activity and ability than in likability

c. rates higher in activity and likability than in ability

d. rates higher in ability and likability than in activity

_____19. If members of a group decide together to take a chance that they would hardly dare take individually, they are exhibiting

a. conformity

b. attitude change

c. risky shift

d. search for consistency

_____20. An individual is *least* likely to conform to group pressure if the

a. individual is a man rather than a woman
b. individual has an "authoritarian personality"
c. other members are in unanimous agreement
d. group is very small

Key to Self-Test

1. (d); 2. (a); 3. (b); 4. (c); 5. (c); 6. (b);
7. (a); 8. (d); 9. (a); 10. (d); 11. (d); 12.
(c); 13. (b); 14. (a); 15. (d); 16. (c); 17.
(d); 18. (b); 19. (c); 20. (d)

exercises

I. If you and your friends have access to two automobiles—one a brand-new luxury car and the other an old, beat-up small car—you can easily try your own version of the experiment described in the text on page 562.*

The purpose of the experiment is to determine the reaction of other motorists to an automobile that remains standing at a stop light after the light has turned green—and especially whether the reaction is affected by the appearance of the automobile. At least two people have to work together in the experiment, first in the big, or "high prestige," car and next in the small, or "low prestige," car. Or four people can conduct the experiment simultaneously, two in each car.

As in the original experiment, it is best to make the trials on a Sunday, in a part of town where traffic is relatively light on that day. The driver of the car arranges to have to stop at as many red lights as possible, in situations where only one other car pulls up behind him and also stops. When the light turns green, he says "Now" to alert his partner but remains stationary. The partner, slumped in the back seat to stay out of view, keeps track of the time that elapses between the "Now" and a honk from the motorist behind. (A stopwatch will give the most accurate readings, but any watch will do.) If there is no honk within twelve seconds, the person with the watch calls "Go" and the driver moves on. A tally can be kept on the chart at the right.

In the original experiment, 84 percent of the motorists who stopped behind the "low prestige" car honked within twelve seconds; only 50 percent

*Doob, A. N., and Gross, A. E. Status of frustrator as an inhibitor of horn-honking responses. *Journal of Social Psychology,* 1968, *76,* 213–18.

of those behind the "high prestige" car honked in that same limit. When the motorist in the car behind was a man, the honk came after an average of about seven seconds for the "low prestige" car and about nine seconds for the "high prestige"

Tally Chart

Time before honk (in seconds)	"Low prestige" car	"High prestige" car
1		
2		
3		
4		
5		
6		
7		
8		
9		
10		
11		
12		
No honk		

car. When the motorist in the car behind was a woman, the honk came after an average of about eight seconds for the "low prestige" car and about eleven seconds for the "high prestige" car. (In computing the average length of time, no honk at all is counted as twelve seconds.) It will be interesting to see how closely your own observations match these original figures.

If enough people can be found to cooperate, the experiment can be enlarged. For example, you can observe the effect of having different kinds of drivers in the two cars used in the experiment; you can see how other motorists react to 1) a teenage male driver, 2) a teenage female driver, 3) a middle-age male driver, 4) a middle-age female driver, 5) an elderly male driver, and 6) an elderly female driver. If the experiment is enlarged in this fashion, it will provide some insights not only into the halo effect of "high prestige" and "low prestige" cars but also into the different norms of behavior motorists have toward drivers of different sex and age.

II. Another experiment in the halo effect can be performed in this fashion: Find a friend who is willing to cooperate with you, and introduce this friend to some people who have never met him before. The introduction can be made to one person at a time or to a group. On some occasions, prepare the people who will meet your friend by telling them something very complimentary about him—that he is very intelligent or witty, or that

he is an exceptional athlete or musician, or that he possesses any other trait that the people are likely to admire. On other occasions, prepare them by making some kind of apology for him; for example, by warning them that he is a bit dull-witted or humorless, or that they will have to watch their step with him because he has a bad temper.

After the meeting, ask them to rate your friend on the scale shown below by checking the appropriate boxes. To get a numerical rating of each person's reactions to your friend, count each check under "very high" as 5, "above average" as 4, "average" as 3, "below average" as 2, and "very low" as 1. The total gives a number representing the general reaction, from a possible high of 25 to a low of 5.

The point at issue, of course, is to determine whether the ratings are more favorable when the introduction has been preceded by a favorable comment than when it has been preceded by an apology. To make sure that your friend's actions do not affect the results, do not tell him how the people he meets have been prepared.

A word of caution: This experiment makes use of deception, which is always a dangerous tool and in fact is considered by some psychologists to be ethically unacceptable in most experimental situations. It is essential that you clear up the deception immediately after you have obtained your ratings. Explain exactly what you have done and why.

Rating

Trait	Very high	Above average	Average	Below average	Very low
Intelligence					
Sense of humor					
Attractive-ness					
Conversation-al ability					
Disposition					